BASIC TEELINE

a textbook of fast writing

BASIC TEELINE

a textbook of fast writing

by

James and I. C. Hill

HEINEMANN EDUCATIONAL BOOKS LTD
LONDON

Heinemann Educational Books Ltd

LONDON   MELBOURNE   TORONTO
AUCKLAND   SINGAPORE   JOHANNESBURG
HONG KONG   NAIROBI   IBADAN

SBN 435 45331 9
Teacher's Book SBN 45332 7

Published by Heinemann Educational Books Ltd
48 Charles Street, London W1X 8AH
Printed in Great Britain by Spottiswoode, Ballantyne and Co Ltd,
London and Colchester

Contents

Acknowledgements

The authors would like to thank Mrs. M. Smith
and Mr. H. Butler, who provided material
for exercises, and the East Midland Educational
Union for permission to use examination
papers.

Preface

This is the first instruction book on Teeline Fast-writing. It follows a 32-page handbook published on 15 July 1968. The handbook was an introduction to a new, untried method of fast writing facing its 'laboratory tests'. The present book is an instruction book based on the results of those tests, on the authors' experience in teaching Teeline, on observation of its effects on students of varying types, and on the experience and reactions of Teeline learners who have become practical writers.

The first experimental classes in Teeline were short courses intended for people who wished to increase their ordinary writing speed for personal use and did not care to spend the many hours necessary to learn one of the traditional shorthand systems which would be far too elaborate for their limited needs. It was found, however, that the simple instruction of Basic Teeline formed a base from which rapid progress to reporting speeds was possible.

Teeline has been demonstrated at two hundred words per minute, but it is still new, and there can be little doubt that even higher speeds are possible.

As Teeline is a method of modifying ordinary writing rather than memorising, increasing speed comes as skill in applying the method increases. Thus the method by means of which words and sentences are written with half the effort of ordinary writing may be applied more intensively to reduce the work still more. The need to memorise long lists of arbitrary short forms does not exist in Teeline: the most advanced forms for words or phrases are simply logical developments from the most elementary Teeline outlines. The Teeline writer may halt his contracting process at any stage adequate for his purpose.

Mental and physical skills are combined in fast writing, therefore thorough practice is needed *at every stage*. This instruction book provides exercises at appropriate intervals to assist digestion of knowledge and consolidate skill along the way. Although the total time and effort needed for Teeline is only a fraction of that required to learn an ordinary shorthand system, the effort put into learning and practice should be not less thorough.

It is the authors' hope that the users of this book may not only reach their high-speed goal, but may also find enjoyment along the way to it.

James Hill
I. C. Hill

1

Introducing Teeline

Teeline is a new way of using an old skill - the skill of writing. Handwriting is a complicated matter which receives our attention in varying degrees from the age of about five. In our later school days we begin to take our manual skill for granted; unless we are unsure of our spelling, our writing becomes as natural a means of expressing our thoughts and feelings as our speech. The great difference is, of course, that we cannot write words as quickly or as fluently as we speak them; the hand appears to be slower than the tongue. Appears to be, but is not really, because the movements are not strictly comparable.

In speech, the tongue and voice are adapted to the needs of the moment, and, measured, the rate of speaking may be anything up to two hundred words per minute and in exceptional cases beyond that speed.

The inability of the hand to keep up with speech or record thought quickly is largely due to the complexity of the movements required to represent words which come simply and quickly from voice and tongue. For instance, in English the simple combined sound of **d** and **o** is written **d o** ugh, and the simple sound of **f** is often represented by **ph** or **gh**.

In seeking the ability to write fast, we are faced with two alternatives: we may learn a new written language which corresponds more nearly to spoken words, (phonographic) or we may adapt the written language we have already spent upwards of ten years learning.

Until the advent of Teeline the first method has been more successfully used than the second because of the difficulties of shortening written words sufficiently for speed whilst retaining their significance.

Teeline removes these difficulties. Words written in Teeline do not need to be translated back into longhand as phonographic shorthand does. They simply require to be expanded or reconstituted, as a pure concentrated extract or essence is diluted back to its natural consistency. The how and why of this process will be found in this book. As unwanted water is driven off in distillation, so the superfluous parts of words are discarded, then the unwanted parts of letters and joining strokes. At this stage, two to three times the normal rate of writing becomes practicable, but it must be realised that only the familiar, unhesitating use of the contracting principles can give speed. Teeline is a skill and like all skills must be practised. In operating a typewriter keyboard, a letter may be struck in a small fraction of a second, but no time is saved if the letter has to be sought.

Why Teeline?

Because the streamlined form of the letter **t** - one of the most common letters - is used as a basis for the contraction and blending of so many words and syllables in English.

Teeline method may be summarised as follows:

1. The omission of unnecessary letters from words.
2. The elimination of unnecessary movements in forming handwritten characters.
3. The blending of characters.
4. The systematic use of common contractions.
5. The abbreviated representation of common speech patterns, sentence clichés, etc.
6. Contracted forms for numbers, fractions, etc.

2
Omission of unnecessary letters

About two-fifths of the characters we ordinarily write are unnecessary. This means most of the vowels and unsounded consonants.

When a word is part of a sentence or 'in context' it is generally easily recognised by its consonantal structure or 'skeleton'. Therefore, except in special cases or when a vowel begins a word, vowels may safely be omitted. For example, the first part of the introduction to this book is printed below, omitting all except initial vowels.

Tln is a nw wy of usng an old skll - th skll of wrtng. Hndwrtng is a cmplctd mttr whch rcvs or attntn in vryng dgrs frm th ag of abt fv. In or ltr schl dys we bgn to tk or mnl skll fr grntd unlss w ar unsr of or spllng or wrtng bcms as ntrl a mns of exprssng or thghts and flngs as or spch.

In many words there are consonants too which are not really needed for recognition of the words, such as unsounded consonants. In Teeline these are omitted. Where doubled consonants occur one is omitted. In the following examples the consonants in brackets are unnecessary and should not be written.

un(n)eces(s)ary c(h)aracter (w)rite al(l) bou(gh) (p)sa(l)m (k)now si(g)n dra(ch)m ni(gh)t (p)neumatic g(h)ost (b)del(l)ium c(h)lorine c(h)rysalis c(h)ronicle c(h)ristian (m)nemonic lam(b) plum(b) clim(b) (ph)thises fil(l)ing fun(n)y tel(l) wrap(p)ing can(n)ot rib(b)ed sud(d)en stif(f)en rig(g)ing ri(d)ge bu(d)ge fe(t)ch ca(t)ch

The combinations **ph** and **gh** are sometimes read and sounded as **f**. When such words are written in Teeline, the **f** character is used. In the following examples all unnecessary consonants and vowels are omitted.

enf = enough   rf = rough   fn = phone   afs = aphis   cf = cough   frs = phrase
flnx = phalanx   fsnt = pheasant   lf = laugh

EXERCISE 2A

Copy the exercise omitting the letters indicated by dots, then re-write in full from your own copy.

Please keep in mind that the manufacture of a final dye often involves the production of numerous intermediate products. For instance, in the case of a certain blue dye required by the Admiralty, we had to manufacture no fewer than six such intermediate materials, none of which were being manufactured in this industry a few years ago. By concentrating our efforts in certain directions we were able to ensure a supply with the result that our Admiralty contractors were never delayed in their work. We are now the sole suppliers of fast blue aniline dye to the Admiralty and our works are now practically self-contained in that we now produce all the complicated intermediate products required for our final dye manufacture.

3

EXERCISE 2B

Write the following, inserting the omitted letters to complete the words.

I mov- th- s-c-nd r-d-ng o- th- L-c-l G-v-rnm-nt B-l-. Th- pr-s-nt p-t--rn o- l-c-l g-v-rnm-nt h-s b—n i- ex-st-nc- f-r m-r- th-n s-v-nty y—rs and th- l-st tw-nty y—rs h-v- s—n r-p-d ch-ng-s i- th- r-sp-ns-b-l-t--s o- l-c-l a-th-r-t--s. C--nc-ls h-v- c-p-d w-l- w-th m-s--v- t-sks f-r wh-ch th-y w-r- n-t d-s--n-d, b-t th-r- is a l-m-t t- wh-t c-n r--s-n-bly b- exp-ct-d. I- is i- th- b-st int-r-sts o- l-c-l g-v-rnm-nt and th- p--pl- i- s-rv-s th-t th-y sh---d c-ns-d-r afr-sh w-t f-rm o- g-v-rnm-nt w---d be b-st s--t-d f-r m-d-rn c-nd-t--ns. Th-t is why th- g-v-rnm-nt h-s s-t up a r-y-l c-m-s---n w--ch w-l r-v--w th- b-s-c str-ct-r- and f-nct--ns o- l-c-l g-v-rnm-nt as s-n a- p-s--bl-.

EXERCISE 2C

Write out the following extract from a speech in full.

Thnk y, Ld Wright, fr yr knd wlcm. I am sncrly tchd by yr wds and b th mnr i wch they hv bn rcvd b th cmpny hr ths evnng. And nw, fr m prt, i cngtlt th Trds Unn Cngrs o rchng its on hndrdth anvrsry. Lkng rnd ths dstngshd asmbly, mtng i ths hstrc Gldhl, i is hrd to blv tht a on tm i ws a crm t blng t a trd unn. Wy ws ths?

Th Cmbntn Acts, a srs o lws dtng frm th mdl ags t th bgnng o th nntnth cntry, hd frwnd upn any cmbnd atmpt t intrfr wth th sply or rgltn o lbr bcs ths ws a fnctn ivstd i the Jstcs o th Pc snc Elzbthn ds. Th Mgstrts hd t dcd wt wgs shd b pd and i ws cnsdrd imprpr fr any bdy or cmbntn o prsns t try t brng prsr t br o thm i th exrcs o thr dty.

EXERCISE 2D

Write out the following, using only the essential letters, then write or read it back from your abbreviated notes.

The Private Secretary

The job of private secretary to a business executive is one of the most important and probably the most discussed in a business office. Just what do business men prize so highly in their secretaries?

The ability to take notes and reproduce them accurately seems to be taken as a matter of course. Most secretaries begin by being shorthand/typists, but the secretary must have other qualities besides office skills. The secretary often knows as much about her boss's business as he does himself. She does not discuss it outside his office: she is discreet and loyal. She is tactful and never intrudes, but when she is needed she is there.

The good secretary does not obviously correct her boss, but she does retrieve his errors when she can, without fuss.

For success as a secretary these things are just a beginning.

4

3
The Teeline Alphabet

The elimination of unnecessary letters reduces the total amount of writing by about two-fifths. The next step is the reduction of movement required in forming the remaining letters. In most cases this means omitting that part of a letter which is not strictly necessary for its recognition. In a few cases writing speed is increased by the method of making the necessary movement.

The Teeline alphabet is set out below. The derivations and explanations for each letter should be carefully studied and the movements practised.

Note: Ruled paper is not essential for Teeline writing, but its use is recommended as it helps to show the position of strokes relative to each other.

Alphabetic Character	Teeline Character	Writing method
A	........▲........	The Teeline **a** is derived from the Roman **A**. Where the full ..▲.. is not necessary or convenient it may be indicated by one of its short strokes, generally .\...
B	6	This is written downwards, with one continuous stroke, a well-defined curve and a bold circle.
C	C	The ordinary form of **c** is written with one movement. It may also be used for the combination ck.
D	∂ or	The full form of **d** is written, like **b**, with a downward movement and a large circle. This form is used *to begin a word.* The short dash for **d** is used in the middle or at the end of a word and is written *below the level of the writing line.*
E	⌐.l.⌐	The full Teeline form of **e** ....⌐.. derives from the Roman **E**. Where the full form is not necessary or convenient it may be indicated by one of its short strokes ..l.. or ..⌐....
F (ph gh)	ℓ𝑔	The ordinary handwritten form of **f** is contracted to a single narrow loop which may be written upward or downward, as convenient. *Note:* **ph** and **gh** when sounded as **f** are represented in the same way.

Alphabetic Character	Teeline Character	Writing method

G (dg) ....ɔ........ The ordinary handwritten form of **g** (*g*) is contracted, and written downward, through the line. The loop *must* be omitted. *Note:* ɔ = dg, as in 'edge'.

H ..../....... Only the downstroke is written and this rests on the line.

I ....ʁ.ɪ.... This must be sloped and acutely angled so that it cannot be mistaken for **v**. Where the full **i** is not convenient or necessary, it may be indicated by its first stroke which is generally written downward.

J ....ʃ......... Written as a single downstroke, through the line, *without loop or dot*.

K (ck) ....⟨......... The straight downstroke is omitted, leaving only the angle. Like **c** this character may be used to represent the combination **ck**

L ....*C*.or.(....... This is a single stroke, boldly curved. It is generally written downward but may be turned upwards for convenience or to avoid writing too far below the writing line.

M ....⌒........ The initial hook and middle stem of the ordinary written **m** are omitted, leaving a single wide arch written from left to right with one stroke.

N ....ᥡ..ᥴ.... The ordinary form of **n** is contracted to the hook or *narrow* arch. The arch must be kept narrow to distinguish from **m**.

O ....ᵕ..ᴑ.... In a few special cases an ordinary full **o** is used: otherwise the indicator. This is the shallow curve at the base of O and should be kept small so as not to be confused with **u** or **w**.

P ....ɪ......... Like the letter **h**, this is contracted to a single downstroke, but while **h** rests on the writing line **p** cuts through it as does the ordinary letter **p**.

QU ....ↄ......... As **q** and **u** are invariably written together, in Teeline the two are blended in one sign. Like **p** this is written through the writing line.

R ....╱......... the ordinary written **r** is contracted to a single upstroke, slanted and slightly elongated.

S ....ᴑ......... The ordinary handwritten **s** is modified to become a circle written as small as convenience allows and in any desired direction.

Alphabetic Character	Teeline Character	Writing method
T	—	This letter is formed by writing only the short horizontal cross-stroke. It is written in the position it normally occupies, i. e. a little above the writing line.
U	u.ı	A simple Roman u written with one stroke. This is like the narrow arch of n reversed and must be written so that it cannot be confused with w or the o indicator. Note that the *indicator* for u is like that for e.
V	V	The upright, angular v, correctly angled so as not to be confused with i.
W	⌣	As in the Teeline m, the middle stem is omitted, making w the reverse of m.
X	X	The traditional cross form of x is used. This is also used for 'ex', as in 'expect', 'express' etc.
Y	U	The ordinary handwritten form of y is contracted by the omission of tail and loop.
Z	℈	Rarely used. The handwritten form of z is reduced to the small first curve with a small circle inside it. It is used only at the beginning of words, the Teeline s being used for z in the middle or at the end of a word.

EXTRA CHARACTERS

SH	S	As the letter S is represented in Teeline by a small circle, the Roman S is used to represent sh as in 'fish' 'wash' 'show' 'she'.
TH	7	This is a combination of the tee cross stroke and the h stroke, forming a single character written in the position of the h stroke.
CH	၄	The Teeline c and h are blended to form one character written in the position of the h stroke.
WH	⌣	Teeline w and h are combined and written in the h position.

Copy the following letter combinations and transcribe into ordinary handwriting.

Vowel indicators inserted, making easier joinings

Letters f and x blended with following or preceding letters

NOTES ON THE ALPHABET

1.   Letters t and d

One of the most frequently occurring letters in written English is t. Because of this frequency it is essential that it should be represented clearly, easily and quickly, and should blend well with other characters. The development of fast writing from these basic points gives this system its name - Teeline.

The letter d is closely related to t in sound and usage, and except when d begins a word, the same sign - a small dash - is used for either t or d.

When a word begins with the letter d the full Teeline d is generally used, e.g. ⟨ ⟩ days, but ⟨ ⟩ aids, ⟨ ⟩ does, but ⟨ ⟩ odes.

The t dash is normally written above the writing line and the d dash below the writing line, but it will be found that it is often safe to join either of these characters to the preceding letter with a consequent increase in facility and speed.

The following examples should be carefully studied:

⟨ ⟩ post,   ⟨ ⟩ had,   ⟨ ⟩ wait,   ⟨ ⟩ speed,   ⟨ ⟩ fat,

⟨ ⟩ food,   ⟨ ⟩ nest,   ⟨ ⟩ but,   ⟨ ⟩ late,   ⟨ ⟩ said.

The common combinations - t-d, d-d, and d-t are indicated by writing the second dash immediately above or below the first, e.g.

⟨ ⟩ batted,   ⟨ ⟩ coded,   ⟨ ⟩ dated,   ⟨ ⟩ mated,   ⟨ ⟩ righted,

⟨ ⟩ raided,   ⟨ ⟩ quoted,   ⟨ ⟩ ended,   ⟨ ⟩ lighted,   ⟨ ⟩ cadet,

⟨ ⟩ waited,   ⟨ ⟩ noted,   ⟨ ⟩ voted,   ⟨ ⟩ stated,   ⟨ ⟩ seeded.

2.   Letter s

The letter s is contracted to a small circle, easy to write and unmistakeable to read. From the reading point of view, the way in which it has been written is immaterial, but speed and facility in writing will be assisted by the following hints:

1.   When s follows a straight-stroke and is itself followed by a second straight-stroke

forming an angle, the circle is best written outside the angle e.g. ⟨ ⟩

2.   When the s circle is joined to a curve it is best written with the same motion as the

curve e.g. ⟨ ⟩

3.   When following ⟨ ⟩ or ⟨ ⟩ the small circle is generally written inside the larger

one e.g. ⟨ ⟩

The Letter x

When a word begins with the sound 'ex' this may be indicated by using the x only, without the vowel, e.g. exclaim ...𝓍... expose ...𝗑... explode ...𝗑... express ...𝗑ₚ...

except ...𝗑... expert ...𝗑‾...

y and i

At the end of a word and, in a few cases, in the middle of a word the letter y has the same use as the vowel i. In such cases the y may be represented by the i indicator, e.g.

ally ...𝓵... wry ...⟋... many ...𝓶... by ...𝟔... fly ...𝓵... . The combination 'oy' should, however, be represented by y only e.g. boy ...𝟔... Roy ...⟋... royal ...𝓎... toy ...ᴜ...

coy ...𝓰ᵤ...

Special use of the 'i' Indicator

The Teeline i ...⟋... written at the end of a word and *disjoined* is used to indicate the word-ending '-ing', thus ...⟋... = paying, ...𝓏... = thing ...𝟔⟋... = being ...∂⟋... = doing

...⟋‾ᵇ... = readings ...⟋ᵇ... = rings

ck: This combination has the hard sound of k and may be represented by either of the two Teeline characters - ...𝗰... or ...𝗸... whichever the writer prefers. To this extent ...𝗰... and ...𝗸... are interchangeable.

c and s

One of the difficulties in recording speech in writing is that the letter c is often sounded exactly the same as s. This occurs in such words as 'peace', 'ace', 'nice', 'race'.

To prevent hesitation in writing or in reading back, the soft c can be written with a small circle inside it to indicate the influence of the s sound, e.g. ...𝓮... ...∂𝓮... ...𝓮...

EXERCISE 3B

Write the following words in Teeline, omitting all *except initial* vowels and non-essential consonants.

about	beef	cod	call	dice	dare
abroad	ball	cough	care	day	dear
bob	bar	cake	case	deaf	does
back	cab	cock	cat	deep	date

fade	fuss	hoax	keg	pick	soap
fig	good	his	lobe	page	Teeline
fame	game	home	lean	pass	vice
folk	gone	head	made	rib	web
fun	gear	joke	man	sob	week
foot	goose	jam	nose	same	well

NOW TRY SUPPLEMENTARY EXERCISES 1 AND 2

SINGLE CHARACTER ABBREVIATIONS

Cassell's *Dictionary of Abbreviations* shows that each letter of the alphabet, standing alone, is used to represent many words of which that letter is the initial. For example, the letter 'a' is commonly used, in different contexts, to represent more than forty different words. Contraction to this extent is not necessary in Teeline writing, but where an initial letter is an obvious contraction in longhand it may be adopted with advantage in Teeline writing. A list of common single-letter abbreviations is given below, and many of these may be used in subsequent exercises.

∧	auto	/	page, population
6	be	ʋ	question, quantity
∂	do, department	/	railway
∟	electric, error	ᵒ	southern
∮	female, feminine	−	to
ᒉ	gentlemen	ʋ	united, upper, you
/	he	∨	very, volts, versus
⟋	I, eye, intelligence	⌣	west(ern), woman
⌐	judge	×	accident
<	king	ᴜ	your
C	letter, lady	7	the
⌒	magistrate, morning	ç	chairman
ᒋ	north(ern)	ʏ	who
ˇ	of	S	shall

11

EXERCISE 3C

Write the following sentences in longhand, copying the Teeline outlines below each sentence.

(1) ....

(2) ....

(3) ....

(4) ....

(5) ....

(6) ....

(7) ....

(8) ....

(9) ....

(10) ....

THE TEELINE ALPHABET

FACILITY DRILL

In exercise 3D and subsequent exercises the following words are used, some of which are contractions. All these words should be practised so that they can be written without the slightest hesitation.

and	_1_	are	_/_	today	_=_	have	_V_	has	_ℓ_

his	_6_	had	_L_	her	_V_	which	_y_	that	_7_

my	_∼_	myself	_𝒸_	on	_1_	can	_ℓ_	not	_2_

me	_∩_	with	_∪_	of	_∨_

Teeline words may often be written more easily and quickly by joining them together, and the frequently occurring groups listed below will be found in the ensuing exercises. In this joining process, it is often an advantage to contract one or more of the words in the group.

Care should be taken not to join together words which do not group naturally in speech or writing, and not to link too many words in one group, as this makes reading back more difficult. The groups listed below should be thoroughly practised.

we have	_∿_	to the	_7_	we will	_℩_	it will	_ℓ_

we are	_∿/_	it is	_ω_	that the	_7̸_	who has (is)	_ℓ_

is not	_℮_	I am	_⌐_	I have	_V_	on the	_7_

with me	_∽_	with the	_7_	we can	_√_	not the	_27_

of the	_7 or 1_	and the	_27_

13

Read, copy and transcribe the following sentences.

(1) [shorthand]

(2) [shorthand]

(3) [shorthand]

(4) [shorthand]

(5) [shorthand]

(6) [shorthand]

(7) [shorthand]

(8) [shorthand]

(9) [shorthand]

(10) [shorthand]

(*Note:* ꝏ = Teeline)

EXERCISE 3E

Put the following words into Teeline:

busy	shop	parcel	curry	kitchen	slipped
office	sold	basket	dinner	roast	quarry
happy	out	dated	already	duck	hurt
garage	Allan	wrote	cooked	cabbage	neck
fetch	well	cake	rice	sago	copy
coffee	bed	thermos	finish	sweet	book
bar	myself	stop	coat	cheese	Teeline
new	please	snack	faded	biscuits	study
yellow	call	cocoa	paid	noon	system
ride	cup	excellent	seaside	girl	fast
lipstick	pills	wipe	dyed	noticed	writing
stock	blue	plates	milk		

FACILITY DRILL FOR EXERCISE 3G

The listed words and groups should be thoroughly practised before attempting the exercise.

chairman, firm, expect(ed), to have, information, February, delivery, alphabet, now, know, no, has been, see, say, so, said, they, what, at, at the, I am sure, I am sorry, special, does not, noon, none, nine, half, accident, let you, have the, which you, you will, had been, into, error, in it

Note: the position of **what** and **at** above the writing line, i.e. in the **t** position. This distinguishes them from **would** and **a** which are written on the writing line.

EXERCISE 3F

Put the following words into Teeline:

fully	quoted	estate	requested	medicine	limited
useful	wife	following	morning	already	tedious
bring	granted	survived	x-ray	studying	right
board	value	goods	causing	vocabulary	first

24 words

Read, transcribe and copy the following:

(1) *[shorthand]*

(2) *[shorthand]*

(3) *[shorthand]*

(4) *[shorthand]*

(5) *[shorthand]*

Note: The full stop may be written upwards for greater speed -

NOW TRY SUPPLEMENTARY EXERCISE 3

4
Blending of characters

It has already been noted that the letter **f** can be blended with other letters instead of being simply joined to them. It will be seen from the examples given on page 8 that a blend of two consonants contains the essential characteristics of each so that both letters are recognisable in the one character.

The principle of blending can be applied to several pairs of letters, forming syllables which can be easily, quickly, and legibly represented. The blends which follow should be carefully studied and practised.

T AND D BLENDS

1. t + r

The **t** stroke (‾) and the **r** stroke (╱) are blended to give one horizontal stroke at least as long as the **t** and **r** strokes joined end to end. This blend will represent - tr, tar, ter, tir, tor, tur(e), etc. e.g.

btr _____ ctr _____ dtr _____ ftr _____ gtr _____ htr _____

jtr _____ ltr _____ ntr _____ mtr _____ ptr _____ qutr _____

rtr _____ str _____ ttr- _____ vtr _____ xtr _____ ytr _____

ztr _____

2. d + r

The horizontal dash for **d** is blended with the **r** stroke, in the same way as the **t** dash, to represent dr, dar, der, dir, dor, etc.

bdr _____ cdr _____ ddr _____ fdr _____ gdr _____ hdr _____

jdr _____ ldr _____ mdr _____ ndr _____ pdr _____ qudr _____

rdr _____ sdr _____ tdr _____ vdr _____ wdr _____ xdr _____

ydr _____ zdr _____

Write the following words in Teeline:

better	bidder	cater	debtor	future	gutter
cedar	dodder	fodder	guider	header	plodder
heater	hotter	jotter	lighter	later	nature
leader	ponder	moderate	radar	reader	tutor
Tudor	voter	extra	sender	finder	wander

Vocalisation of t and d and their blends

To make reading easier, vowel indicators may be attached to t and d and their blends as follows:

bat ...6... batter ...6... bet ...6... better ...6... bit ...6...

boat ...6... boater ...6... but ...6... butter ...6...

3. t + n

Teeline letters t ...... and n ...1.. are blended as shown - t + n = ...7... This blend forms syllables tan, ten, tin, ton, tun, tion, etc.

bitten ...6... cotton ...6... eaten ...... fatten ...6... mutton ...6... motion ...6...

potion ...6... portion ...6... lotion ...6... ration ...... notion ...6...

The dash form of d may be blended with n in a similar way to the t -

bidden ...6... cadence ...6... Eden ...... hidden ...... laden ...6... London ...6...

4. t + r + n

The double blend, t + r + n, giving syllables tren, tron, trun, train, tarn, tern, tirn, torn, turn, etc. is formed by blending tr (—) with n (1) thus - ⌐, and the similar combinations of d + r + n are written by blending dr with n, thus - ....

bittern ...6... turn ...... return ...... pattern ...... stern ...... veteran ......

restrain ...... train ...... trend ...... trundle ...... trinity ...... trinket ......

distrain ...... postern ...... electrons ......

NOW TRY SUPPLEMENTARY EXERCISES 4 AND 5

18

5. c blends

The letter c is blended with other characters as follows:

c + m =   ...C.... company ...⌐... common ...⌐... commit ...C̄... commence ...⌐...

campaign ...⌐... camel   ...C... camber   ...C... commerce ...C...

c + n =   ...C... contain ...C... consume ...C... contact ...C...

c + n + v =   ...√... converse ...√... convict ...√... convivial ...√...

c + n + tr =   ...C... contract ...C... contrary ...C... centre   ...C...

c + m + tr = ...C... cemetery ...C... commuter ...C...

c(k) + t(d) = ...C... cooked ...C... fact   ...R... wrecked ...✓... elect ...✓...

c(k) + tr(dr)= ...C... factor ...R... elector ...✓... sector ...C... lecture ...✓...

6. n blends

n + p =   ...?... nap   ...?... snip   ...9... nipple ...7... nape   ...?...

n + v =   ...√... never ...√... invoice ...√e... knaves ...√... naval ...√...

n + x =   ...X... next ...X... inexperienced ...X...   Nixon ...X...

7. p blends

p + b =   ...b... publish ...b... piebald ...b... republic ...b...

p + v =   ...√... poverty ...√... pave ...√... pavane ...√... Pevensey ...√...

p + x =   ...✗... pixie ...✗... pax   ...✗...

NOW TRY SUPPLEMENTARY EXERCISE 6

8. r blends

r + f = ... rough   .... reef   .... ref(erence)   ....

r + k = ... rake   .... barracks   .... park   ....

r + x = ... Rex   .... Pyrex   .... Corrux   ....

9. v blends

v + l = ... value   .... vale   .... volt   ....

v + n = ... vain   .... even   .... vantage   ....

v + r = ... verge   .... vertical   .... versify   ....

v + x = ... vixen   .... cervix   ....

10. w blends

w + f = ... wife   .... waif   ....

w + k = ... week   .... woke   ....

w + n = ... own   .... known   .... brown   ....

w + r = ... ewer   .... our   .... bower   ....

w + r + k = ... work   .... were   ....

w + x = ... wax   .... *Note* - waxworks   ....

NOW TRY SUPPLEMENTARY EXERCISE 7

11. Vowel blends

The vowel combinations **ou** ...⤵... and **oo** ...⤴.... may be blended to give ...⤳... (the Teeline **w**), and like the simple vowels, this indicator may be included in or omitted from a word as required.

Special applications of blends

The syllables con, coun, can, com, cum, cam, etc. often follow en-,   e-,   un-,   in-. When this occurs the first syllable is represented by a vowel indicator

economics		unconfirmed	unconfined
unconsidered		inconsiderate	incontinent
encounter		incompetent	encompass
incomplete		incommode	encumbrance

NOW TRY SUPPLEMENTARY EXERCISE 8

Joined blends

As the writer becomes familiar with the use of the **t** and **d** dashes and their blends it will be found that it is often safe to join either the **t** or **d** to the preceding character, with consequent increase in facility and speed, e.g.:

fast		faster		bidder		cider		bed	
bedder		better		debtor		hint		hunter	
rent		render		find		finder		sender	
mender		patter		actor					

FACILITY DRILL FOR PRACTICE
BEFORE EXERCISES 4B and 4F

last time		tête-a-tête		best time		bringing the	
our, were		about the		it would be the			
we were		with the		are not		but	
with it		will be		can you		public	
should be		too		in fact		on to the	
accidental		if you have		from		behalf	
owes		tattoo		was		speech	

EXERCISE 4B

Read, copy and transcribe the following sentences:

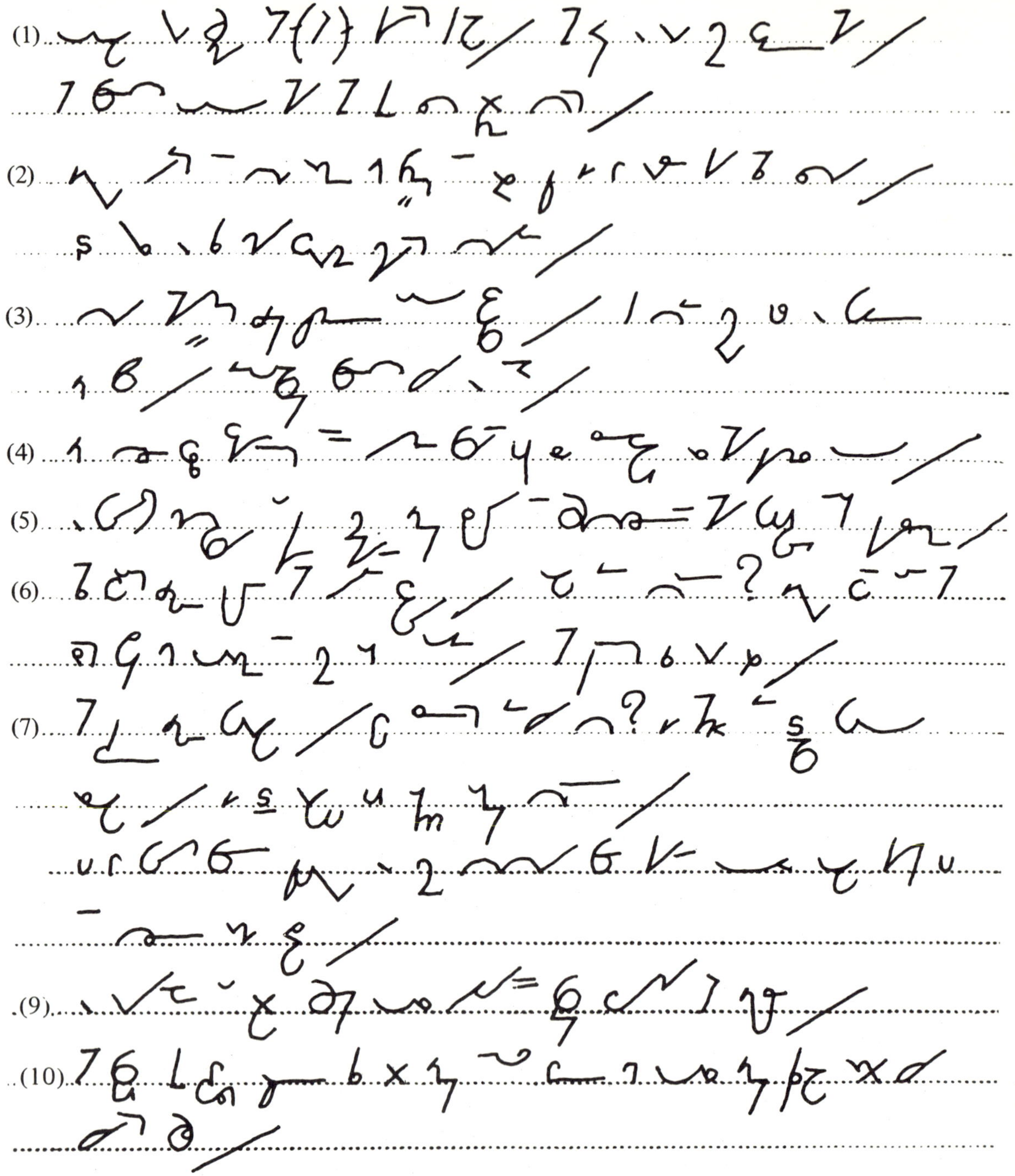

BLENDING OF CHARACTERS

EXERCISE 4C

Put the following words into Teeline:

Hilton	Garden	parents	want	learn	concussion
cider	Market	demonstrate	pattern	work	town
mutton	Thornton	President	picture	master	centre
written	lecture	cotton	level	accidental	annexe
London	children	matter	straighten	coroner	fourteen
Covent	strictly	satin	lower	inquest	

35 words

EXERCISE 4D

Put the following words into Teeline:

signed	parts	attended	rector	bringing	workman
sending	motor	matins	annoyed	refrained	completely
Rudd	scooter	Trinity	quite	commenting	knocked
excite	tarnished	Te-Deum	tête-a-tête	vintage	feeling
interest	paint	Latin	rudely	quite	dreadful
include	Peter	extract	interrupted	potent	routine
yacht	decided	Exodus	waiter		

40 words

EXERCISE 4E

Put the following words into Teeline:

enquiry	pavilion	padre	wanton	offenders	fishing
contract	unveiled	volcano	vandals	instead	beaten
behalf	war	poverty	reduced	turning	reef
company	veteran	village	volume	blind	wind
involved	Tattoo	volunteers	active	water	waited
refused	week	combat	spotting	rough	Neptune
findings	squadron	invading	reporting		

40 words

EXERCISE 4F

Read, copy and transcribe

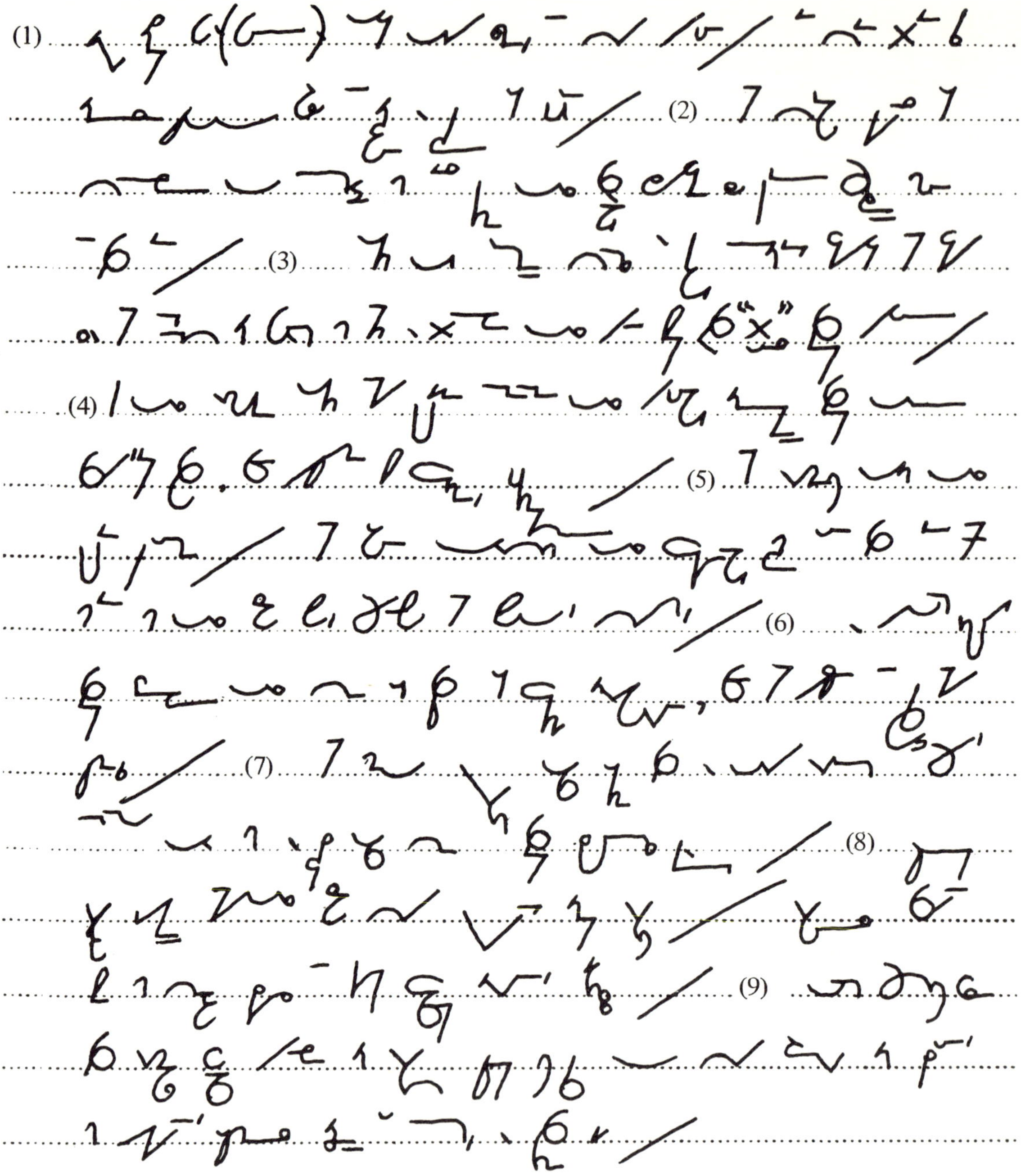

5
Word beginnings and endings

under-

In the word 'under' and its compounds syllable un- is contracted to the single letter **u**, as follows :   understand ......   understood ......   under-dog ......

undertake ......   under-tow ......   under-signed ......   under-pin ......

self

The word 'self', used as a prefix, is contracted to sl .... This is generally joined, but disjoining is safe: self-evident ......   selfish ......   self-coloured ......

self-denial ......   self-interest ......   self-possessed ......   self-controlled ......

trans

When writing the syllable 'trans-' the **n** may safely be omitted for greater facility and speed: transact ......   transfer ......   translate ......   translucent ......

transpire ......   transubstantiation ......

WORD ENDINGS

-ing The contracted form of the syllable ing has already been shown, and several other common endings are likewise contracted to single characters or combinations:

-ang ⎞
-ong ⎟ as for - ing, the vowel indicator for
-eng ⎟ **a, o, e,** or **u** is generally disjoined
-ung ⎠ but written close to the
      preceding letter.

bang ......, rang ......, hang ......, sang ......, wrong ......, song ......,

long ......, strong ......, prong ......, bung ......, lung ......, strung ......,

clung ......, dung ....

25

Notes

(a) Teeline s may be added to -ng signs

things ...7...... , longs ...6...... , bungs ...6b...... , sings ...96...... , songs ...9.9...... .

(b) The addition of a second -ng is indicated by an additional tick:

ringing ...../"..... , singing ...9u....... , banging ...6.x...... , longing ...6.y...... .

(c) Other letters or characters may be added to ng:

strongly ....C.., wrangle ..../l....., bangle ...6).... , singly ...9.... , strength ....7.. .

NOW TRY SUPPLEMENTARY EXERCISE 9

-tation ⎫
-dation ⎪ These common endings are represented by a variation of ...⊃... tn and ......dn.
-tition ⎬ To indicate the extra syllable the n ...∩... is joined but not blended,
-dition ⎭ thus ...⊃... = -tion, but ...∩... = -tation, -tuition, -tuation

affectation ...r∩..., superstition ...p∩..., erudition .../∩...,

accommodation ...C∩.., station ......∩..., situation ...e∩... .

EXERCISE 5A

Put the following words into Teeline:

understand	completely	understudy	economy	comment	counterfoil
undergraduate	constantly	concert	income	intended	contrast
accommodation	quarrelling	accompanies	consider	action	self-reliant
extremely	nuisance	contralto	own	transfer	convince
uncomfortable	unconfirmed	council			

27 words

EXERCISE 5B

Put the following words into Teeline:

accomplished	constant	irritating	hesitation	important	expedition
composed	banging	bangle	strongly	addition	lungs
songs	trying	rings	recommending	exposed	recommendation
nothing	things	longing	content	irritation	strengthen
irritation	consideration	country	trade	connection	contract

30 words

-able -ability -ible -ibility -oble etc.	These endings are indicated by writing the appropriate vowel – *not the indicator* – disjoined, immediately after the root word – desirable ⟨⟩ deplorable ⟨⟩ capable ⟨⟩ durable ⟨⟩ table ⟨⟩ treble ⟨⟩ edible ⟨⟩ likeable ⟨⟩ sensibility ⟨⟩ gullible ⟨⟩ indictable ⟨⟩ lovable ⟨⟩ noble ⟨⟩
sh-l tial cial	All these endings are spelled differently and may therefore be written differently in Teeline - sh-l ⟨⟩ tial ⟨⟩ cial ⟨⟩ but as they are all sounded like sh-l they may all be represented by the Teeline character ⟨S⟩ (sh) generally disjoined - partial ⟨⟩ martial ⟨⟩ marshall ⟨⟩ crucial ⟨⟩

Note: A vowel may be added

- partially ⟨⟩ specially ⟨⟩

NOW TRY SUPPLEMENTARY EXERCISE 10

-ology -ological -alogy -alogical	The full letter **o** is written close to the root word but disjoined and above the normal level of writing. biology ⟨⟩ genealogy ⟨⟩ psychological ⟨⟩ zoology ⟨⟩ sociological ⟨⟩ physiological ⟨⟩ meteorological ⟨⟩
-ologist	This is formed by adding the Teeline s and t to the -ology 'o' biologist ⟨⟩ sociologist ⟨⟩ psychologist ⟨⟩ zoologist ⟨⟩
-ward -word -wood	Write Teeline 'w' in the 'd' position, i.e. below the normal level of writing - inward ⟨⟩ eastward ⟨⟩ crossword ⟨⟩ upward ⟨⟩ backward ⟨⟩ redwood ⟨⟩ plywood ⟨⟩
-ment	Teeline **m**, which may be reduced in size, is written in the t position - payment ⟨⟩ instalment ⟨⟩ experiment ⟨⟩

-mental Teeline **l**, which may be reduced, is added to the '**ment**' sign.

instrumental .... elemental .... experimental ....

-mentary Teeline **r** added to '**ment**' - elementary .... supplementary ....

NOW TRY SUPPLEMENTARY EXERCISE 11

-graph
-graphy The **r** is omitted and the **f** is blended with the **g.** Note the use of the vowel indicator to show the -y ending. photograph .... photography .... pantograph .... heliograph .... autograph ....

Note the use of .... as abbreviation for prefix '**auto**'.

-gram The **r** is omitted from between **g** and **m** - radiogram .... pictogram ....

NOW TRY SUPPLEMENTARY EXERCISE 12

EXERCISE 5C

Put the following words into Teeline:

bank	supplementary	frequently	seaward	expressions	bang
payment	allowances	trouble	hopelessness	queued	table
consignment	position	cheerfulness	situation	autograph	programme
self-willed	investments	nobility	horribly	controversial	educational
accomplishments	biologist	themselves	sensible	report	archaeology
admiration	capable	photograph	laughable	committee	zoology
situation	temperamental	specially	fatuousness		

40 words

FACILITY DRILL FOR EXERCISES 5D, 5E, 5F

they must have been	to do	income
that she is	subjects	come
some people	order	we should
I think	frequently	before
further	season	enclose(d)
complete the	session	that they are
round	committee	but there
form or firm	to see	newspaper
who has	off	long time

business	business *(shorthand)*	there is	there is *(shorthand)*	exchange	exchange *(shorthand)* or *(shorthand)*
with the matter	with the matter *(shorthand)*	to be	to be *(shorthand)*	though	though *(shorthand)*
become or became	become or became *(shorthand)*	account	account *(shorthand)*	calm	calm *(shorthand)*

EXERCISE 5D
Read, copy and transcribe

(1) *(shorthand outline)*

(2) *(shorthand outline)*

(3) *(shorthand outline)*

(4) *(shorthand outline)*

(5) *(shorthand outline)*

(6) *(shorthand outline)*

(7) *(shorthand outline)*

EXERCISE 5E

Read, copy and transcribe

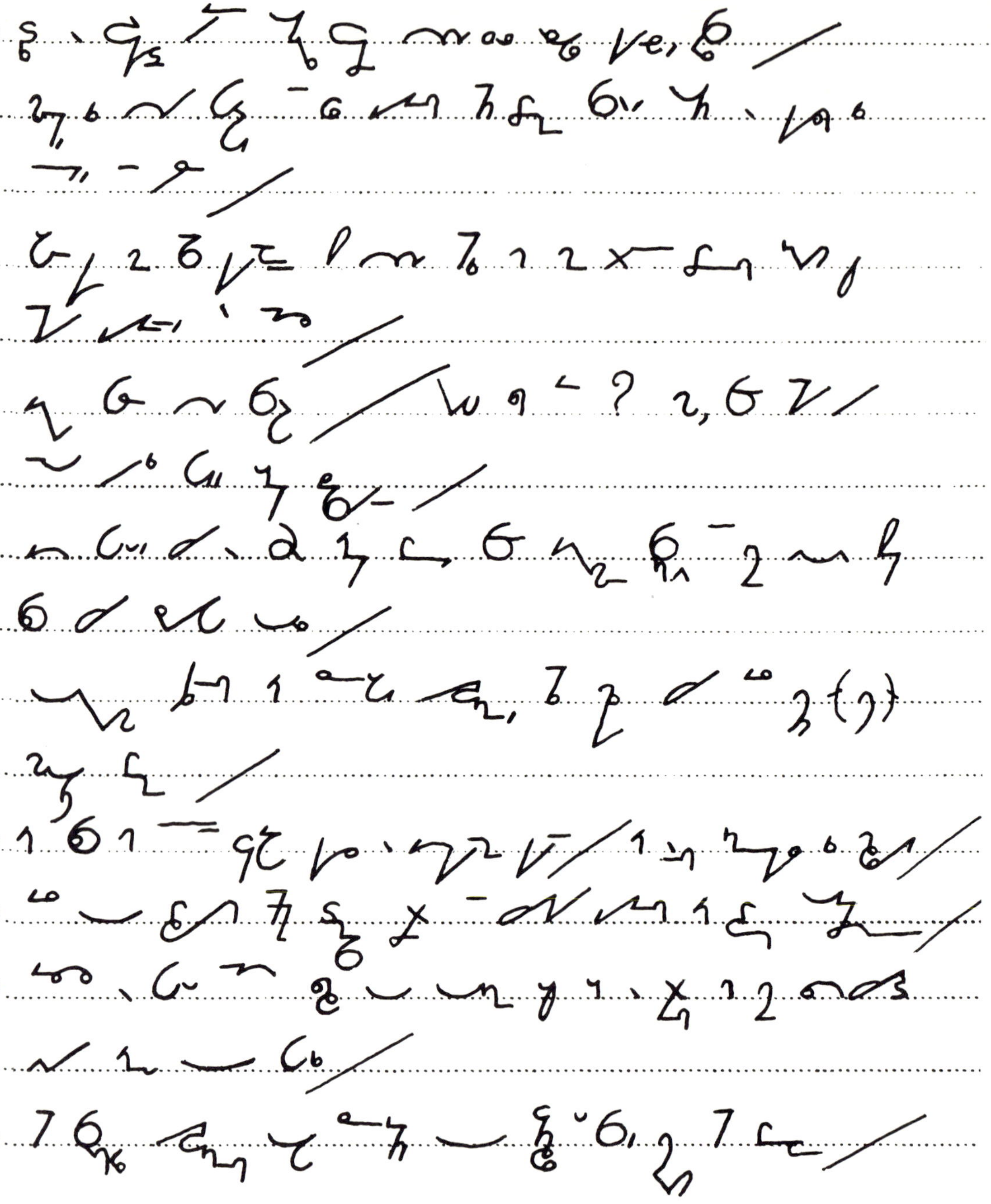

(1)

(2)

(3)

(4)

(5)

(6)

(7)

(8)

(9)

(10)

EXERCISE 5F
Read, copy and transcribe

(1) ....

(2) ....
....

(3) ....
....

(4) ....

(5) ....
....

(6) ....
....

(7) ....
....

(8) ....

(9) ....
....

(10) ....
....

6
Word groupings

In foregoing exercises, words which join together easily in Teeline have been linked in groups. This process of grouping words in speech and writing is a natural one, and Teeline method allows full advantage to be taken of it.

Two words may be used together so often that in writing they become linked by a hyphen, then even the hyphen disappears and the two words merge into one, e.g. 'extra ordinary' becomes 'extra-ordinary' then 'extraordinary'. In speech, especially colloquial speech, the process is more common, less obvious and more insidious, and when a verbal joining becomes established it finds its way into writing and print, e.g. the well-known 'pinta', 'cuppa', and 'teach-in', 'break-out', 'beating-up', which will become 'teachin', 'breakout' and 'beatingup'.

Whole sentences may become so much units of speech or writing that the beginning engenders in the mind an expectation of what is to follow. Thus, when a speaker says 'And last, . . .' we expect 'but not least' or . . . 'but by no means least'. Businesses and professions have their own clichés and repetitive speech patterns and the Teeline writer should observe them and match them with appropriate written patterns or outlines.

The really intensive study of condensed groupings is necessary only for the very high-speed writer, but simple group patterns are within the scope of the most basic Teeline writer. They should be (a) easily written, (b) easily recognised, (c) natural groupings. No linked group should take longer to write than the separate words, or lose legibility because of the joining.

The groups in the following facility drill relate particularly to Exercise 6A, but the method should be carefully studied and generally applied.

FACILITY DRILL FOR EXERCISE 6A

Words

Word		Word		Word	
without		intermission		transitory	
interfere		undersigned		contrary	
introduce		underdogs		automobile	
entertainment	or	thoroughly		concept	
suitable		undergone		maintenance	

32

proceedings		underground ... or ...	favourably
receptive		transpired	orthodox
element		transaction	brown
television (TV)		undertaken	movement
relaxation		intentions	automatic
ourselves		nothing	

Groups

with the arrangements		I must point out	
it would appear		that it would be	
for example		by means	
some form of		this is no	
and we must		which would	
have been		make sure	
some of the		those days	
may be considered		best interests	
whole arrangement		few months' time	
methods of transport		in addition	

EXERCISE 6A

Read, copy and transcribe

(1)

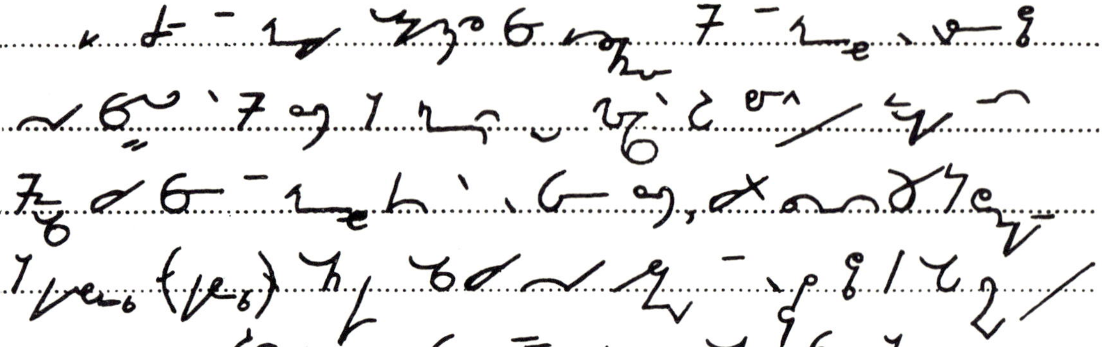

(2)

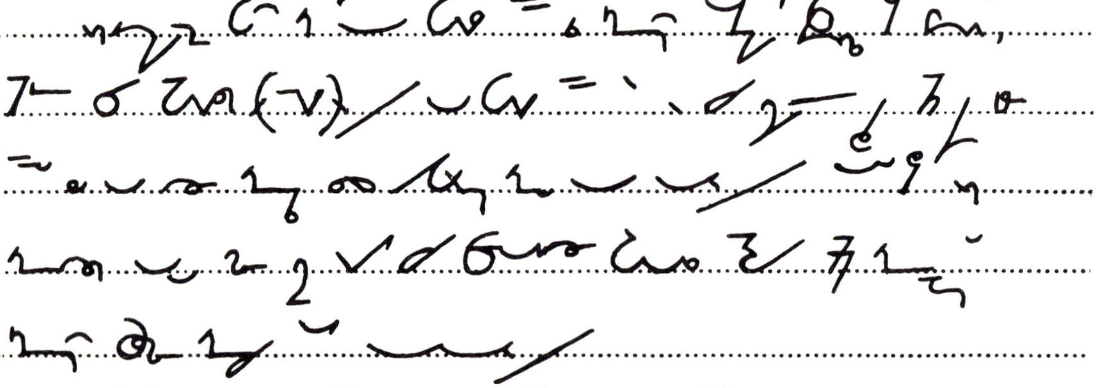

(3)

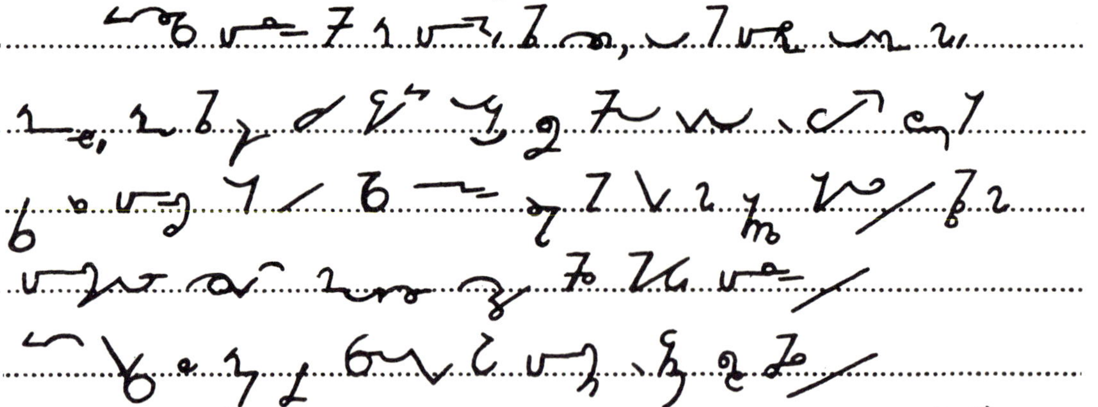

(4)

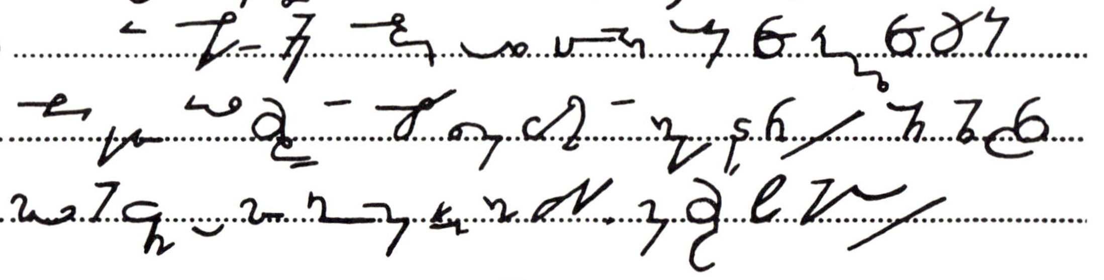

(5)

(6) (a)

(b)

(c)

(d)

(e)

(f)

(g)

FACILITY DRILL FOR EXERCISE 6B

Words

policeman	social	sufficiently	doubted
improvements	self-defence	everything	

Groups

for the council		acting in the interests (of)	
said the matter			
use of their		general public	
of them		presented with the	
present state		annual general meeting	
country's economy			
young man		long and happy retirement	
police station		last night	
make a statement		made the	
before us			
we would say		on behalf of the members	
for instance		and they were sorry	
counsel for the defence		it was now	
summing up		from time to time	
congratulated the		they would see	
who were		no doubt	

36

EXERCISE 6B

Read, copy and transcribe

(1) ....

(2) ....

(3) ....

(4)

7
Numbers and fractions

The ordinary Arabic numerals are a kind of fast writing to which everyone is accustomed, and although faster methods are possible, ordinary figures are generally adequate from one to ninety-nine. It is in writing round numbers that effort is generally wasted, and the following simple devices will eliminate this waste.

(a)   In writing *hundreds* use the **dr** blend (equivalent to 00) written under the hundreds figure: 2 = 200,   3 =300,   5 = 500

(b)   For *thousands* use the **ths** blend (equivalent to 000) *enlarged* in the **t** position close to the numeral - 4 = 4,000,   7 = 7,000

(c)   For *hundred-thousand* use a blend of **dr** and **ths** under the appropriate numeral(s)
      - 2   = 200,000,   12   = 1,200,000

(d)   For *million(s)* use **m** close under the appropriate numeral - 1 = 1,000,000
      12 = 12,000,000.

(e)   For *hundred-million* write the combination of **dr** and **m** under the appropriate numeral - 4   = 400,000,000.

(f)   For *thousand-million* use the combination of **ths** and m - 6 = 6,000,000,000.

Note: 'Per cent' is indicated by writing Teeline **p** ( ) close to the relevant

numeral - 4 = 4%   Instead of using the 'pound' sign (£) the word 'pounds' should be indicated by Teeline **pd** - 8 = £8, 6 = £600

Common fractions

The most commonly used fractions - half, quarters and thirds - are indicated in conjunction with numerals as follows:

Fraction	Character	Examples
half		= 1½, = 2½, = 3½, = 4½, = 5½,
		= 6½, = 7½, = 8½, = 9½, = 10½,

Fraction	Character	Examples

quarter — ^{U}

1^U = 1¼, 2 = 2¼, 3^U = 3¼, 4 = 4¼, 5^U = 5¼,
6^U = 6¼, 7^U = 7¼, 8 = 8¼, 9^U = 9¼, 10^U = 10¼,

three-quarters — ^{U}

1 = 1¾, 2 = 2¾, 3 = 3¾, 4 = 4¾, 5 = 5¾,
6 = 6¾, 7^U = 7¾, 8 = 8¾, 9 = 9¾, 10^U = 10¾,

Third — ^{L}

1^L = 1⅓, 2^L = 2⅓, 3^L = 3⅓, 4 = 4⅓, 5^L = 5⅓,
6^L = 6⅓, 7^L = 7⅓, 8^L = 8⅓, 9^L = 9⅓, 10^L = 10⅓,

NOTE = 33⅓

two-thirds

1 = 1⅔, 2 = 2⅔, 3 = 3⅔, 4 = 4⅔, 5 = 5⅔,
6 = 6⅔, 7 = 7⅔, 8 = 8⅔, 9 = 9⅔, 10 = 10⅔,

Notes: (a) In 'three-quarters' it is necessary only to show the plural of 'quarter', by adding s.

(b) In 'two-thirds' it is necessary only to show the plural of 'third' by adding a further tick.

FACILITY DRILL FOR EXERCISE 7A

thank you for your letter (of the)    during the year

for your order (of the)    this year

would you

40

EXERCISE 7A

Transcribe the following sentences:

(1) [shorthand outlines]

(2) [shorthand outlines]

(3) [shorthand outlines]

(4) [shorthand outlines]

(5) [shorthand outlines] 850

(6) 1971 [shorthand outlines]

(7) [shorthand outlines]

(8) [shorthand outlines] 6,130 [shorthand outlines] 35 [shorthand outlines]

8
Insertion of vowels

An analysis of many thousands of words of connected matter showed that the number of words which needed vowels to be shown was less than two per cent. In the natural flow of Teeline writing a much greater number of words than this contain vowel indicators, making reading easier. Nevertheless, provision must be made for every possible contingency, and in rare cases the insertion of a vowel or vowels in an outline which has been written without them may be desirable.

(a) to distinguish between words which have the same consonantal structure, when the context is not a sufficiently good guide.

(b) to give an indication of the spelling of the word, especially a name or an isolated word.

(c) to indicate more fully the structure of an unfamiliar word.

An inserted vowel is written close to the consonant with which it is associated.

The vowels and indicators are given the following significance:

.....ʌ....   is the 'name' sound as in 'pale', 'pate', 'mail', 'fail', 'fate'.

.....ˎ.....   is the short sound as in 'pal', 'pat', 'cat', 'fat', or as in 'pall', 'mall', 'call', 'fall'.

.....┗....   is the 'name' sound as in 'peel', 'peak', 'leak', 'feel', 'heal', 'steal' etc.

.....ˎ......   is the short sound as in 'pet', 'peck', 'hell', 'dell'.

.....ʌ....   is the 'name' sound as in 'like', 'pile', 'ripe'.

.....ˎ....   is the short sound as in 'lick', 'pick', 'rip', 'pill'.

.....O....   is the 'name' sound as in 'pole', 'bole', 'sole', 'goal'.

.......ˇ....   is the short sound as in 'Polly', 'dot', 'cot', 'spot'.

.....ɣ....   is the 'name' sound as in 'Yŭle', 'gule', 'dupe', 'mule', 'cupid'.

.....ˈ.....   is the short sound as in 'gull', 'mull', 'cup', 'sup'. This looks like the e indicator, but confusion is not likely to occur in use.

It should be remembered that the insertion of vowels is rarely necessary, but must be a practical possibility.

To deal with a need which is still more rare, if the writer wishes to record the unusual lengthening of a vowel, this may be done by repeating the indicator, thus - **a-ah** = ...ˎˎ...., **ee-e** = ...ˎˎ... , etc.

VOWEL COMBINATIONS

Each of the five vowel letters in the alphabet has its Teeline equivalent, and each of the Teeline vowel characters or its indicator can be joined to every other vowel character or indicator. This process is rarely necessary, but should be used with facility and legibility if required, and for reference a chart showing the best joinings is given below.

aa	ae	ai	ao	au
ea	ee	ei	eo	eu
ia	ie	ii	io	iu
oa	oe	oi	oo	ou
ua	ue	ui	uo	uu

Note: These characters are slightly enlarged for extra clarity.

EXERCISE 8A

Transcribe the following Teeline words into longhand, showing the spelling which is represented by the Teeline vowel signs.

9

Additional abbreviating methods

Letters **b, c, d, g, p** are often combined with letter **r** without the insertion of a vowel between them, e.g. **br, cr, dr, gr, pr**. Thus, when **r** immediately follows **b** and the two letters are not separated by a vowel, the Teeline **r** becomes a short stroke *inside* the **b**. This short stroke may be blended with the following letter, as follows:

br .... (brew or brow) becomes ...., ... (bream) becomes ....

brittle = ... broad = ...

If the character which follows the **r** is **s**, the **s** circle is written inside **b**

thus - .... **brs** (British Road Services).

If the letter following the **r** is a vowel, the indicator may be written inside the **b**:

bra .... : bre .... : bri .... bro .... : bru ....

Compare - bars ...., with brass ...., Bert ...., with Brett ...., ... bored

.... with broad.   *Note:* .... bring.

cr The same method may be applied to **c + r**, e.g. cr-b .... cr-f .... cr-g ....

cr-k .... cr-l .... cr-m .... cr-n .... cr-p .... cr-r .... cr-w .... cra ....

cre .... cri .... cro .... cru ....

> *Note:* carve ....   certain ....   curd ....
> but   but   but
> crave ....   cretin ....   crude ....

dr This blending will apply to the initial **d** (........) only.

.... drab .... drake .... dread .... dreary .... dram .... drape

gr .... great .... grand .... gray .... grow .... grip .... grim.

> Compare - grill .... with girl .... grid .... with gird ....

44

pr Letter **p** may be intersected to indicate a blended **r** promise .... protect ....

produce .... provide .... prince ....

Note: production = ... or ....

When intersection of the letter **p** is not practical, the presence of letter **r** may be indicated by writing the following stroke close to the **p**:

press .... proceed .... propose .... prehensile ....

a o u Letter **r** may be indicated with these vowels by writing the following letter through the vowel: arrange .... art .... argue .... order .... orange .... oracle ....

urge ....

Note: the vowel **a** enlarged (.Λ.) may be used for the word or prefix **arch**:

arch ....Λ.... arch-bishop .... arch-criminal ....

Abbreviation of tion, sion, cian, shion, etc.

This frequently occurring syllable, generally pronounced **sh-n** may be contracted by writing it as the hook form of **n** disjoined but close to the preceding letter -

fashion .... magician .... elocution .... distribution ....

selection .... ocean ....

FACILITY DRILL FOR EXERCISE 9A

British Rail	....	in reply	....	in spite (of)	....	dear sir	....
credit sales	....	after dinner	....	over the year	....	yours faithfully	....
part of the	....	references	....	enclose	....	expect	....
they do not	....	with reference (to)	....	we thank you	....	expected	....
during the year	....	take steps	....	for your letter	.... (........)	awkward	....
cup of tea	....	raw materials	....	with your letter	....	profit	....

(1) .....

(2) .....

(3) .....

(4) .....

(5) .....

(6) .....

(7) .....

(8) .....

(9) .....

(10) .....

(11) .....

(12) 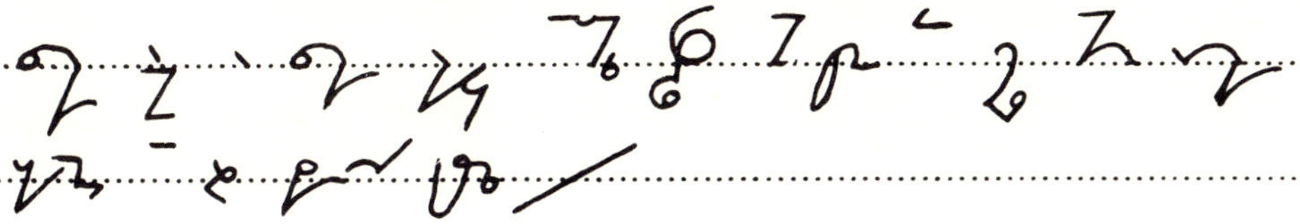

(13) 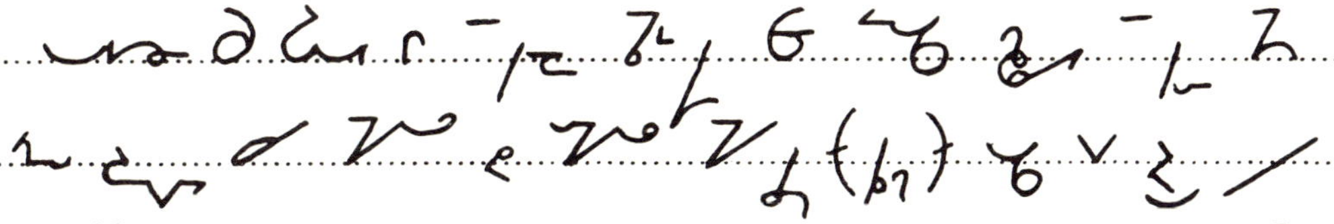

(14) 

(15) 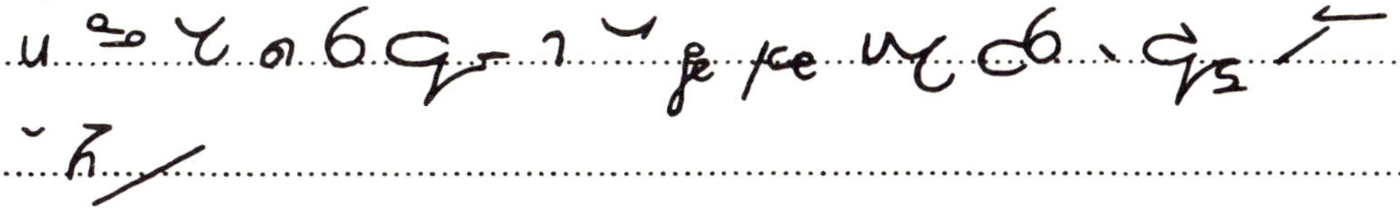

(16) 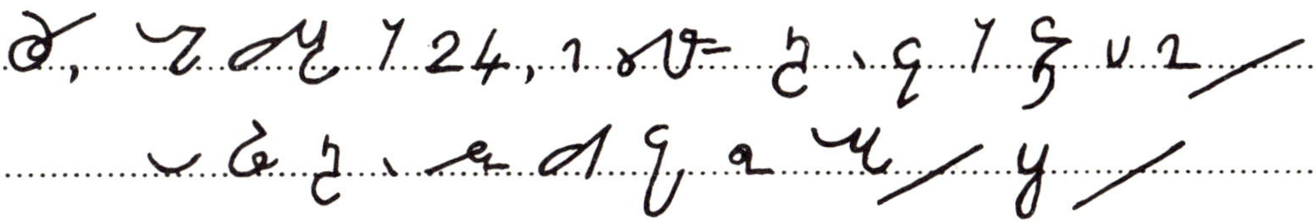

FACILITY DRILL FOR EXERCISE 9B

co-operation	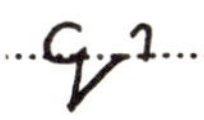	research staff		reduced cost	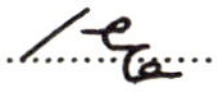
generations		in the way of		two weeks	
quality		fully justified		we can	
unfortunately		centuries ago	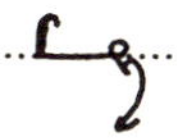	prompt attention	
thought		commonplace book	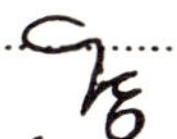	circumstance	
gentlemen		long letters		owing	
number of		with you		attitude	
about the position		last consignment		yesterday	

await		in the circumstances	
complimentary remarks		we are pleased to know	
open minds		assuring you	
they required		at all times	
leaders of industry		particulars	
far-sightedness		handwriting	
considered to be		consignment	
in reply to your letter (of)		communication	
we regret to inform you		immediately	
and we feel			

EXERCISE 9B

(1)

(2)

(shorthand outlines)

(3) *(shorthand outlines)*

(4) *(shorthand outlines)*

FACILITY DRILL FOR EXERCISE 9C

old-established	*(outline)*	rather	*(outline)*
representative	*(outline)* or *(outline)*	furthermore	*(outline)*
telephone	*(outline)*	with this letter	*(outline)*
given	*(outline)*	discount for cash	*(outline)*
turnover	*(outline)*	during the year under review	*(outline)*

on account		plant and machinery	
foreign side		early part of the year	
we regret to state		coming year	
for the year		United States	
directors' report		lower than	
declare a dividend		it has been	
board of directors		United Kingdom	
under separate cover		we are sending you	
take this opportunity		your earliest convenience	
we should be pleased		best attention	
in the course of his speech			

(1)

(2)

(3)

(4)

EXERCISE 9D

Write the following passage in Teeline, using suitable word groupings:

Advertising Policy

For some time we have been considering a complete change of policy in selling our goods. We propose from next month to advertise in a number of trade papers which we have not hitherto used for this purpose and to experiment with colour advertisements. In addition, we intend to distribute posters advertising special offers to the local supermarkets. We shall be pleased if there is any way in which you feel we could further increase our output. We need to treble our takings during the year and are therefore running a competition for ideas. A competition form is enclosed with this letter. The closing date for its receipt is Friday, September 3rd.

EXERCISE 9E

Write the following passage in Teeline, using suitable word groupings:

Noise is one of the greatest problems of the present time. Everyone agrees that the volume of noise increases yearly; but not everyone agrees about what constitutes a noise. To the motor-cyclist, the sound of an engine throbbing may be music. His view is not shared by the woman with a headache, outside whose window he parks, chatting with his friends above the din. A dog, yelping with excitement on being allowed into the garden to chase the birds, may amuse his owner, but it is no laughing matter for the shift worker across the way who has just been woken by it from a snatched day-time rest. The television set, blaring at the end of a hospital ward for the interest of convalescent patients, is a positive nightmare to the really sick person who only wishes to sleep.

Scientists have discovered that working constantly in a noise frequently causes deafness. Intense noise can even damage the ears, and doctors say that much mental illness today is caused by living in a noisy environment.

It is a surprising thing, therefore, to discover that most people seem to like noise. Some even carry it around with them in the form of a transistor radio. In fact, those who complain about noise, and seek peace and quiet, are often considered to be cranks.

GROUPED INITIALS

Single-letter abbreviations generally require a context to make them precise in their meaning; for example, the letter **b** standing alone may mean almost any word beginning with **b**. In a group, however, its possible meanings are narrowed, and two **b**'s in the same group may help to define each other. In an advertisement **b** and **b** could reasonably be either 'bed and breakfast' or 'bed and board', depending on the wider context in which it is seen.

Many initial-groupings make sense only in a specialised vocabulary, and will be used and understood only by people accustomed to the jargon or clichés of some particular business or profession. Thus **d** and **d** used in a magistrate's court will mean 'drunk and disorderly' to the court reporter, the policeman - and to the habitual offender, but would probably be meaningless to a commercial office clerk. The group c & f on the other hand, meaning 'cost and freight', will be familiar to the clerk and probably mean nothing to the policeman.

The Teeline writer should build up a relevant list of initial groupings for his own purposes by reference to a standard dictionary of abbreviations or a specialised trade list, converting the longhand initials into Teeline characters and joining them when practicable. The examples listed below should be carefully studied and the appropriate ones practised.

GROUPED INITIALS

Group	Teeline	Meaning
A & A		additions and amendments
A.C.		advisory council
BB		Boys' Brigade
BC		borough council
b/d		brought down
b/f		brought forward
b & s		brandy and soda
b/l		bill of lading
BR		British Rail
c.o.d.		cash on delivery
C.o.E.		Council of Europe
CD		Civil Defence

53

Group	Teeline	Meaning
DJ		Disc jockey
d & p		developing and printing
d.a.p.		documents against payment
GP		general practitioner
HQ		headquarters
HP		hire purchase, horse power, hardy perennial
JP		Justice of the Peace
LG		local government, ladies and gentlemen
m & b		mild and bitter
p.a.r.		planed all round
v.g.		very good
GM		General Manager

EXERCISE 9F

Read the following exercise, write it in Teeline, using the Teeline versions of the longhand abbreviations, then write it in full longhand.

They say the G.M. won his C.M. when he rescued his office char after a G.M. explosion. He is quite a char himself and v.g. academically: he is a B.Sc.(Econ.), M.A.(Oxon), and gained a Ph.D. for a thes. on some aspects of Mod.E. At one time he was a V.I.P. on the B.B.C. and I.T.V. and when he was M.P. for Luton, Beds., some of his colls. expected him to become P.M. or Ch. and a member of the C.o.E. He was, of course, a communicant of the C. of E. and had been Amb. to an E.F.T.A. country.

Appendix

ALPHABETICAL LIST OF WORDS FREQUENTLY USED IN THIS BOOK

able		British		eastward		
about		British Rail		easy		
accident		British Road Services		enclose/d		
accidental		business		error		
and		but		Europe		
arch		buy/by		exchange/d		
archbishop		came come		expect		
are		can		expected		
at		chairman		eye		
auto		circumstance		February		
awkward		communication		few		
be		crossword		firm form		
became become		deliver		for		
before		delivery		frequently		
behalf		do		from		

55

full	*ℓ*	Mr.	per cent
further		never	policeman
general	.).or .)	newspaper	pounds
gentlemen		next	production
given		noon / none	profit
go		north / northern	public
half		northward	quality
has		now	question
have		of	rather
his		off	reference
I		on/one	references
immediate		or	representative
immediately		order	round
improvements		our	say
income		out	see
inform/ed		owes	self-defence
information		owing	session
letter		own	shall
me		particulars	social

special		to		were	
speech		today		what	
subjects		too/two		which	
sufficient		turnover		who	
sufficiently		unfortunately		with	
telephone		United Kingdom		would	or
that		United States		year	
the		U.S.A.		you	
they		very		your/yours	
though		was		zero	
thought		we			

5

Supplementary exercises

SUPPLEMENTARY EXERCISE 1

Copy and transcribe the following

(1) ....

(2) ....

(3) ....

(4) ....

(5) ....

(6) ....

(7) ....

(8) ....

(9) ....

(10) ....

(11) ....

(12) ....

(13) ....

(14) ....

(15) .... [Teeline shorthand] ....

SUPPLEMENTARY EXERCISE 2

Write the following words in Teeline:

1. abase Ann any ape apex beef book baking bars beam boy
2. calling car carry caves caving coy dumb dope dear daring dared
3. elf emerge enclose encourage each earl fan funny fag fish fuss folk
4. gained gaping gears gas gem gulley hen honey home hat hit haste
5. ice image idle it if Jack join jar James jeered jelly
6. kale keep keg kill kiss kissed leaping loom lair less last loop
7. me meet marry make mum mummy neck not need knocked nose nearest
8. old off ox ogle opera picking picket pens pass past pushing
9. quarry quarrel quake quick quest quail rug rake roast rich rip wretch
10. said sell slick skill stitch sorry toffee take tale tow teaspoon twice
11. viper vote voting vast visit vex would wig waste wait weeks weather
12. chain change charge check chair cheque chaff chop child church
13. thigh think thought thick them thesis there thorn throb thence
14. when whip whether where why whisk whisper whim while whiskey
15. shave ship shame shine shrew shrimp shrink shirk show shot
16. Feb. fable fabulous fabric febrile fly flow flip flue flick
17. fame family famish female fumble far fry Friday fern frantic freak
18. half haft gaff myself himself rough reefs quaff waif housewife
19. express expel exam. excel ex-ray hexagon lax mix pax Rex
20. yeast matted dated raided rated stated staid study studied
21. rust rusty rusted esteem estate estimate aspire most wasp sleep
22. despair despaired bestow listed slices sweet flames ban bin been

SUPPLEMENTARY EXERCISE 3

Put the following sentences into Teeline:

1. We-will let-you-have the faulty piece of cloth when we have examined it. Please see what you can do about-the marks. (24)
2. By-the end of-this-week you-will get-the book for-which you asked. (15)
3. We-can go on-the bus if-you do-not-wish to drive in-this rainy weather. (17)
4. I-am-sorry that-the special delivery you expected did not arrive, but I-am-sure it-will-be at-the depot today. (23)
5. Half the road was flooded when the car crashed into-the van at-the crossroads, but-the damage to both vehicles was slight. (23)

6. The P.M. will arrive at Party H.Q. at / noon on Monday. He will have lunch at H.Q. / and-then visit the new G.P.O. buildings. He / is expected to leave by car at nine p.m. /   (40)

7. The slim blond was asked to take a film test in America.   (12)

8. Please inform the Personnel Manager that the firm's senior representative / is-not now in London. He-is in Italy buying / leather goods. We-have a good sale for Italian handbags / in Derbyshire. This representative is a Derby man himself.   (39)

9. Have you managed to gain any information which-will be of use to-the firm? (15)

10. The Chairman said he would-be at-the office each morning during this week. (14)

SUPPLEMENTARY EXERCISE 4 **(f blends)**

Write the following in Teeline:

1. The last time we saw him was in February. It / would be when we were going to the seaside. He / followed us on to the train, but made for the dining / car and we lost sight of him after that. It / was a very full train and we had to stand / most of the way to Blackpool. (56)

2. He thrust the flowers into my hand and fled. The / beautiful scent from them filled the air. Memories of the / past flooded back to me and my eyes filled with / tears. (31)

3. There are few things I like better than strawberry flan. / For days I had tried to stifle my appetite, but / this was too much for me. I accepted a large / slice and ate it greedily. (35)

SUPPLEMENTARY EXERCISE 5 **(tr, dr, tn, dn, trn, drn** blends)

Write the following in Teeline:

1. You will have a better future with Teeline as an extra skill.   (12)
2. The missing trinket was found in the gutter.   (8)
3. The bittern's eggs are hidden near the cedar tree.   (9)
4. The actor returned to London on the train.   (8)
5. We must fatten the geese for Christmas by increasing their rations. (11)
6. The fox ran faster as the hunters drew near.   (9)
7. I find this lotion very good for the skin when the weather gets hotter. (14)
8. Can you find me an easy pattern for making up this material?   (12)
9. He was by nature a moderate eater.   (7)
10. The modern trend is to cater for the teenager.   (9)

SUPPLEMENTARY EXERCISES

SUPPLEMENTARY EXERCISE 6 (c, n and p blends)

Write the following in Teeline:

1. The camber of the road is an important factor in safe driving. (12)
2. After they had consumed the champagne they became more convivial. (10)
3. He was convicted of committing a felony. (7)
4. The lecture contained some facts never before made public. (9)
5. Do you have a contract with this company? (8)
6. The factory was not far from the city centre. (9)
7. Can you introduce me to the naval officer we met at the tattoo? (13)
8. Please extract the copies of this firm's invoices from our files and bring them to me this afternoon. (18)
9. We learn more from experience than we do from parents or teachers. (12)
10. A feature of the new motor car is that it will turn easily in a limited space. (17)

SUPPLEMENTARY EXERCISE 7 (r, v, and w blends)

Write the following in Teeline:

1. We were on our own last week and would have welcomed company. (13)
2. My wife cut her hand when she broke the Pyrex dish, and it has not yet healed. (17)
3. Too much work has brought him to the verge of a breakdown. (12)
4. Although there is no difference in the food value of / brown and white eggs, most people in this country choose brown. (21)
5. It is a well-known fact that wax forms a protective covering for leather boots. (15)

SUPPLEMENTARY EXERCISE 8 (Special application of blends)

1. How inconsiderate of the Chairman it was to allow the / meeting to continue after the stated time. The speaker had / to return to London that evening. (26)
2. Economy is a good thing, provided it is not carried / to extremes. To economise on necessities and buy luxuries instead / is foolish. (22)
3. After our encounter with the tiger, I was glad we / had brought the rifles, although at first I had regarded / them as an encumbrance. (24)
4. The motorist was given an unconditional discharge when the evidence regarding the accident had been considered. (16)
5. With his usual incompetence, he has handed in an incomplete report on the flower show. (15)
6. The activities of the inconspicuous little man were inconsistent with the incoming reports. (13)

7. The incompetence of these inconsiderate employees is unconfirmed. (8)
8. The incumbent regarded the study of economics as unconsidered and incongruous. (11)
9. The inn sign 'Goat and Compasses' is said to come from the incomplete rendering of 'God encompasses us'. (17)

SUPPLEMENTARY EXERCISE 9 (under, self, trans, ing, etc.)

1. I understand the business is being transferred to a new company. (11)
2. Some-people think that-she-is selfish, but I-am-not so sure. (13)
3. This season we intend to use our own transport when we attend the song sessions. (15)
4. Can you translate this newspaper article into German for me? I frequently need matter in that language. (17)
5. If-you can manage to transport these goods from our / warehouse we-can let-you have them at a reduced / cost. (21)
6. It takes a strong will to undertake a course of / dieting and stick to it until the desired results are / obtained. (21)
7. As-we came round the corner, we shouted with all / our strength, but-the answering call now seemed to-be / farther off. (22)
8. You had better ring them up and make-sure they / are going to-be in before we deliver the goods. / (20)
9. If-we-feel it-would-be useful to-have an / exchange of ideas, we-will call a meeting of-the / committee members before-the end-of-the month. (28)
10. At one-time, singing was considered to-be an art / for which a long training was necessary. Today, anyone / who can make a noise is called a singer and / fame can come easily in a short space-of time. / (40)

SUPPLEMENTARY EXERCISE 10 (tation, able, sh-l, etc.)

1. When we got to the station we had to wait / a long-time for the train as the time-table / had been revised the week before and we had not / realised the change affected us. (36)
2. Superstition has a strong hold on many people. They cannot / walk under ladders or spill salt at the table without / expecting bad luck. (23)

3. It is desirable that children should be taught the difference /[10] between poisonous berries and those which are edible. It is /[20] natural for small children to taste everything they see, and /[30] this frequently brings disastrous results. (35)

4. I think she has obtained a new situation on the /[10] staff of the local newspaper. This does not seem to /[20] be a suitable job for such a gullible person. (29)

5. Although he admitted his misdemeanour, he did not realise that /[10] he had committed an indictable offence. (16)

SUPPLEMENTARY EXERCISE 11 (ology, ward, ment, etc.)

1. At one time doctors studied only physiology, but today a /[10] good doctor takes the psychology of his patients into account /[20] when prescribing for their ailments. (25)

2. Many people would like to investigate their family tree, but /[10] genealogical search is a long and expensive business. It must /[20] be very interesting to be a genealogist. (27)

3. The meteorological office is now commonly referred to as the /[10] 'Met' office. This modern tendency to shorten names would have /[20] been frowned upon at the beginning of the century. (28)

4. Some families buy too much on the instalment plan. In /[10] order to keep up with the payments they go short /[20] of necessities. This is a deplorable situation. (27)

5. In spite of her apparent affectation I find her very /[10] likeable, and she has been most capable in her handling /[20] of our recent experiments. (24)

SUPPLEMENTARY EXERCISE 12 (graph, gram, etc.)

1. Speaking for myself, I thought the programme boring. It was /[10] too elementary in its approach to the subject under discussion. /[20] (20)

2. In this photograph she is looking upwards. You can see /[10] much better than in the other how sensible she looks. /[20] (20)

3. They bought themselves a radiogram as it is clear /[10] that-they-are going to be spending a lot of /[20] time on their-own in the future, and this will /[30] help them to pass the time during the long winter /[40] evenings. (41)

4. A heliograph may be an engraving obtained by exposure to /[10] light, an apparatus for photographing the sun, or a signalling /[20] apparatus reflecting flashes of sunlight. (25)

5. They say the new automatic car drives itself. Some people /[10] do not find this desirable. They prefer to be in /[20] charge of the automobile. (24)

SUPPLEMENTARY EXERCISE 13 (Teeline)   *Time*

Transcribe the following passages:

(a) [Teeline shorthand outlines]

(b) [Teeline shorthand outlines]

SUPPLEMENTARY EXERCISE 14

Put the following passages into Teeline:

A. Harvesting the produce is the part of gardening I like / best. Fresh-gathered vegetables, cooked and eaten as they are / required, have a taste which cannot be equalled by any / bought ones. Even cabbage becomes delicious in these circumstances.
      Unfortunately, / before the harvest can be enjoyed, much hard work and / careful thought must be put in. Not everyone is prepared / to do this in order to eat like a king. /   *(70 words)*

B. Dear Friend,
      Once again we appeal for your continued support / in our fight against poverty.
      We enclose an illustrated brochure / of the cards we are offering this Christmas. Last year / the sale of cards broke all previous records. Supplies are / immediately available, and overprinting of your name and address can / be speedily carried out at a small extra charge as / shown in the list.
      Our Christmas seals will brighten your / letters and parcels while helping to swell our funds.
      We / hope to receive an order from you,
                                    Yours sincerely,   *(89 words)*

C. We should like to draw your attention to the fact / that your subscription to our magazine is due to expire / next month. If you desire to continue as a reader, / please let us have your contribution before the end of / this month. If on the other hand, you wish to / cancel your order, please complete and return the attached slip / as soon as possible.
      We hope we may continue to / rely on your support and that you will inform us / if you are not entirely satisfied with what we offer. /   *(90 words)*

D. For some time we have been considering a complete change / of policy in selling our goods. We propose from next / month to advertise in a number of trade papers which / we have not hitherto used for this purpose, and to / experiment with colour advertisements.

SUPPLEMENTARY EXERCISE 14 (contd.)

In addition, we intend to distribute ⁵⁰/ posters advertising special offers to the local supermarkets. We shall ⁶⁰/ be pleased if there is any way in which you ⁷⁰/ feel we could further increase our output. We need to ⁸⁰/ treble our takings during the year and are therefore running ⁹⁰/ a competition for ideas. A competition form is enclosed with ¹⁰⁰/ this letter. The closing date for its receipt is Friday, ¹¹⁰/ September 3rd. *(112 words)*

GENERAL BUSINESS EXPRESSIONS

dear sir	your letter	with reference
dear madam	herewith	enquiry
dear sirs	quotation	enclose(d)
dear sir or madam	in your reply	
I have your letter (of)	in reply to your letter	
we have your letter (of)	by return post	
we have received your letter (of)	postal order	
we acknowledge receipt of your letter (of)	money order	
we thank you for you letter (of)	urgently required	
with ref. to your letter (of)	in confirmation of telephone call	
referring to your letter (of)	your order	
In payment (of)	thank you for your order	

66

in payment of account		this account is now overdue	
your account		prompt payment	
statement of account		prompt attention	
monthly account		yours faithfully	
general manager		yours truly	
managing director		very truly yours	
sales manager		yours sincerely	
works manager		company secretary	
chairman and managing director		yours respectfully	

SUPPLEMENTARY EXERCISE 15

Write the following in Teeline:

There are still traditional ways of beginning a business letter although many of the hackneyed phrases in daily use only a few years ago have now almost completely gone out of use. We still start a business-letter with dear-sir, dear-sirs, dear-madam, or gentlemen, followed by such phrases as in-reply-to-your-letter, we-have-your-letter, thank-you-for-your-letter, or with-reference-to-your-letter. At the end of the letter we still use yours-faithfully, yours-truly, very-truly-yours, and more rarely yours-obediently or yours-respectfully.

The vocabulary of general business contains many references to enquiries, quotations and orders, often in such phrases as - in-reply-to-your-enquiry (of) 24th June, we-have-pleasure in giving below our quotation. . . . There are many letters about accounts, invoices and statements, containing such phrases as in-payment-of-account, statement-of-account, monthly-account. Orders too are often mentioned and we say - my-order, your-order, our-order and, of course, postal-order or money-order, sometimes asked for by-return-post.

Letters are sometimes written in-confirmation-of-telephone-calls or messages, and the term urgently-required is often used when referring to delivery of goods.

SUPPLEMENTARY EXERCISE 16

Write the following business letters in Teeline:

1. Dear Madam, Thank you for your letter of 13th September /¹⁰ concerning Glow-warm vests. We are, however, unable to be /²⁰ of assistance in this matter, as this product has been /³⁰ withdrawn from sale and is not now manufactured. We regret /⁴⁰ that we are unable to help you further.

Yours faithfully,   (50)

2. Dear Sirs, Thank you for your note of 9th September, /¹⁰ advising us of the return of 84 pairs of rompers /²⁰ which were delivered to you in error. Credit has been /³⁰ passed for the amount of postage, and a credit note /⁴⁰ will reach you during the next few days. We should /⁵⁰ like to take this opportunity to thank you for return-ing /⁶⁰ the goods.

Yours truly,   (64)

3. Dear Madam, Thank you for your recent letter concerning a /¹⁰ sleeping suit purchased as a gift for your son. Normally /²⁰ we do not exchange garments, but in the circumstances, if /³⁰ you will return this garment we will replace it with /⁴⁰ a larger size. There will, of course, be a slight /⁵⁰ price adjustment, plus return postage,

Yours faithfully,   (57)

4. Dear Sir, I have your letter of last Monday, and /¹⁰ note your remarks concerning the non-collection of your refuse. /²⁰ The matter has been taken up with the department concerned /³⁰ and I trust that you will have no further cause /⁴⁰ for complaint.

Yours faithfully,   (44)

Write the following letters in Teeline:

1. Dear Sir/Madam, Your staff and students are invited to / attend an exhibition in the Drill Hall, High Street, demonstrating / the use of the most modern types of office equipment. / This is not a collection of competing brands of what / is essentially the same machine but rather a glimpse of / the office of the future. If you are interested in / automatic mailing systems, microfilm filing, document reproduction, automatic dictating equipment, / accounting machines, internal communication systems, office furniture, automatic typewriters, computers, / etc., you will be interested in our exhibition. The use / of closed circuit television as a teaching and training / aid will also be demonstrated.
The exhibition will be open from / 10 a.m. to 6.30 p.m., Monday to Friday, 4th / to 19th November inclusive.
It is suggested that students be / allowed to visit the exhibition in class time, and special / arrangements can be made for parties on request.

Yours faithfully,   (150)

2. W. A. Goodwell, Esq., Organising Secretary, Business Efficiency Exhibition.
Dear / Sir; Thank you for your letter of 24th October inviting / my staff and students to the Business Efficiency Exhibition. This / should be very interesting and instructive, and I will ask / class tutors to make arrangements with you by telephone for / visits by small groups of students accompanied by teachers.

Yours faithfully,   (61)

SUPPLEMENTARY WORD AND GROUP LIST

ACCIDENT = X

the accident	_X_	bad accident	_6/X_
an accident	_xX_	fatal accident	_ftX_
this accident	_2/X_	nasty accident	_2/X_

serious accident		day of the accident	
slight accident		time of the accident	
car accident		scene of the accident	
motor accident		noise of the accident	
domestic accident		cause of the accident	
works accident		since the accident	
similar accident		immediately the accident happened	
engineering accident		the accident happened	
flying accident		before the accident	
railway accident		prior to the accident	
accidental	or	following the accident	
accidental death		as a result of the accident	or
accident black spot		witness(ed) the accident	
caused an accident		saw the accident	
caused the accident		number of accidents	

after the accident ....T.7......... previous accident ....✗......

after an accident ....T......... accident report form ....✗......

accident report ....✗......... accident prevention committee ....✗......

SUPPLEMENTARY EXERCISE 18

Write the following in Teeline, using the special word groupings indicated.

Accident Reports

The firm's accident-prevention-committee are extremely concerned at the / increasing number-of-accidents in the Company's factories. The committee / have, therefore, designed a new accident-report-form, and you / will be required to complete this accident-report-form as / soon as possible after-an-accident.

The details required will / be, the date of the accident, the time-of-the-accident, / whether it was a serious-accident or a slight- / accident, and the cause-of-the-accident if known. Find / out if the man has suffered a similar-accident prior- / to-the-accident reported and if he has been involved / at any time in a railway-accident, a flying-accident / or even a domestic-accident. State where he was before / the accident and what he did immediately-the-accident-happened, / and give details of the work the man was doing / when-the-accident-happened. Interview all who were near the / scene-of-the-accident, but bear in mind that the / noise-of-the-accident can confuse people who saw-the-accident. / Say if you have taken any steps since-the-accident / to adjust any machinery damaged as-a-result-of-the-accident. / In the factory any works-accident is likely to be / a nasty-accident, but an engineering-accident can very easily / become a fatal-accident. Please help us to ensure that / we never have to record a verdict of accidental-death. (230)

Local Government List

administration		works and open spaces com.	
administrative		baths committee	
county council		civil defence	
county districts		appeals committee	
non-county districts		welfare services com.	
county borough council		consultative com.	
municipal(ity)		advisory com.	
municipal council		town planning com.	
urban district council	UT or UC	your committee	
rural district council	T or C	this committee	
parish council		rating and valuation com.	
metropolitan boro' council		rateable value	
corporation		gross value	
boundary commission		housing scheme	
housing committee		mayor	
housing department		deputy mayor	

health department		mayoress		N.B. mayors
health committee	or	deputy mayoress		
finance committee		town clerk		
finance department		deputy town clerk		
public health committee		town clerk's department		
public health department		borough surveyor		
works committee		borough surveyor's dept.		
public works com.		clerk to the county council		

SUPPLEMENTARY EXERCISE 19

Write the following Local Government pieces in Teeline, using the special local government groupings and contractions:

1. Every journalist should be familiar with local-government and the / various local-government-departments. He may need to report the / meetings of a county-council, a county-borough-council, a / metropolitan-borough-council, urban-district-council, rural-district-council or / parish-council. The reporter also needs to be familiar with / the various committees and departments, such as the housing-committee / and the housing-department, the town-planning-committee, watch-committee / and baths-committee. Generally there is a public-health-committee, / and certainly sooner-or-later the reporter will need to / write about the finance-committee or finance-and-general-purposes- / committee. Then there is often a welfare-service with its / welfare-service-committee and it will often be necessary to / refer to the mayor or mayoress and to various local- / government-officials such as the town-clerk, the clerk-to- / the-county-council, borough-surveyor, borough-treasurer, city-engineer, etc. (150)

2. Our-committee was divided in its opinions. The deputy-town-clerk / said that-the motion should not have been put to the / housing-committee and certainly should never have appeared in the minutes / as a resolution of that-committee. He had no doubt / that after the next meeting of the town-planning-committee / the whole matter would be reviewed and the offending minute / would be rescinded. He had discussed-the-matter with the / town-clerk and the clerk-to-the-county-council who / agreed that the whole matter was no more than an / error in procedure which could and no doubt would / easily be rectified. (103)

INSURANCE AND RELATED EXPRESSIONS

insurance	Royal Exchange
accident insurance	underwriters
accident insurance company	renewal of policy
personal accident insurance	life assurance
bad debt insurance	building society
insurance policy	all over the world
British insurance companies	invisible exports
fire insurance	banker's order
marine insurance	claim for compensation
motor vehicle insurance	distribution of surplus
personal injury	burglary insurance

forms of insurance		third party insurance	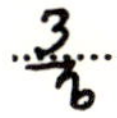 or 
house insurance		contingency insurances	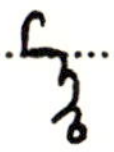
car insurance		contract of indemnity	
compulsory insurance		legal liability	 or 
personal negligence	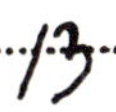	contributory negligence	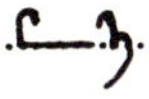
employers' liability act		workmen's compensation act	 or 
court of appeal		in the course of his employment	
temporary total disablement		permanent injury	
wilful misconduct		permanent disablement	
bodily injury		partial disablement	
totally incapacitated	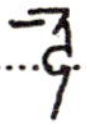	form of proposal	

SUPPLEMENTARY EXERCISE 20

INSURANCE

Put the following passage into Teeline:

Insurance forms an important part of a country's invisible exports. / British Insurance companies, for instance, obtain three-quarters of their / business from foreign customers. The probable reason for their success / overseas is that they are known and trusted all over / the world. Insurance is, after all, built on trust. In / return for the money you pay to an insurance company / you receive only a promise to pay compensation in the / event of some disaster overtaking you.

Some forms of insurance / are compulsory - for example, car insurance, and if
you are / buying your home through a building society, house insurance. No-one, /
however, is compelled to insure his own life, though most / people do, largely for
the benefit of their dependents.

The / first fire insurance company was formed after the Great Fire / of London,
in the 17th Century. As there were no / local fire brigades in those days, the
insurance companies had / to employ their own.

Marine Insurance, for the protection of / ships and cargoes, began earlier, and
in the reign of / Queen Elizabeth the First, the Royal Exchange, in London, was /
the headquarters of the underwriters who handled this.

Nowadays, most / people think of Lloyd's as the world centre for shipping /
insurance, although its business is much broader in scope. It / is interesting to
remember that this was originally a fashionable / coffee house in the time of
Samuel Pepys. No-one visualised, / in those days, the National Insurance schemes
we have today. /

(240 words)

COMPANY MEETINGS AND REPORTS

Frequently occurring phrases

annual general meeting		annual turnover	
annual review		in the course of his speech	
at the moment		in the meantime	
balance of payments		increased profit	
current year		in my review	
cut production		increased taxation	
competitive position		margin of profit	

SUPPLEMENTARY EXERCISES

chancellor of the exchequer		gross profit of the group
debt of gratitude		group trade
due to		great achievement
distribution methods		operations of the group
distribution and sale		overseas companies
extract from the statement by the chairman		overseas trade
end of the year		board of directors
the following is an extract		policy of your board
future prospects		report and accounts
level of profits		reduced profits
most important		corporation tax
general reserve account		raw materials
final dividend		interim dividend
subsidiary companies		capital expenditure
		board of trade

(See specimen examination papers, pages 110-118.)

The key to this exercise counted for dictation is on page 106.
Read and copy:

Nottingham Goose Fair

[shorthand outlines]

Rule Britannia

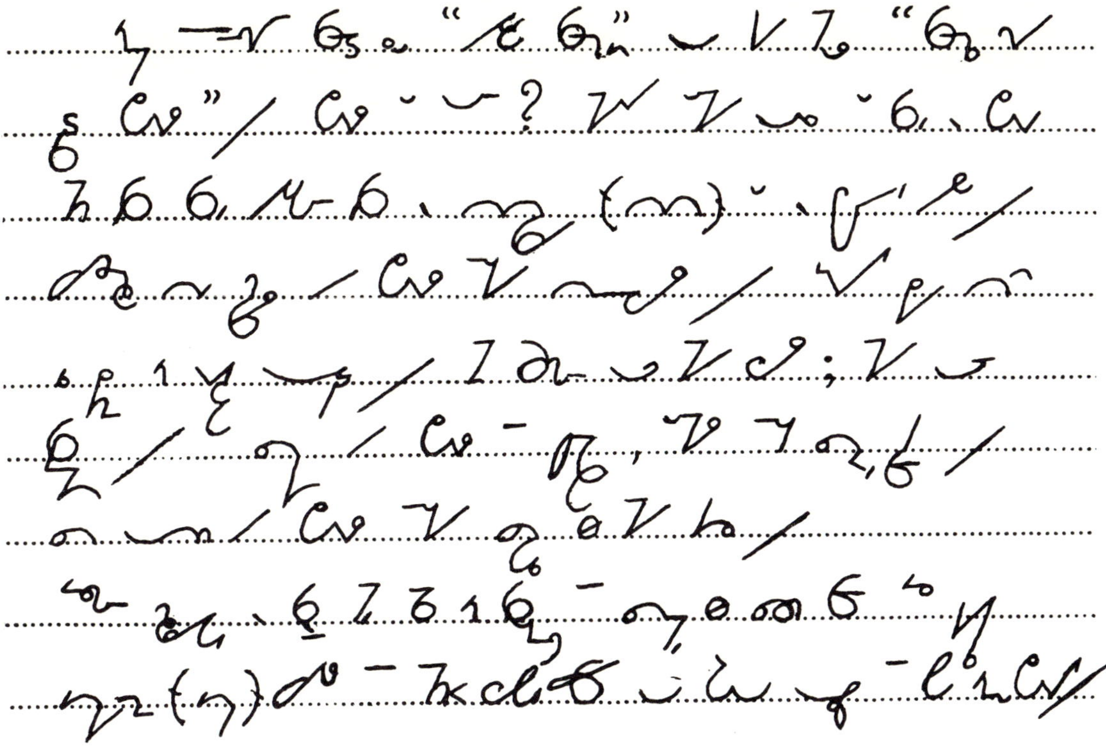

[Shorthand text]

SUPPLEMENTARY EXERCISE 22

Read and copy:

The private Secretary (2)

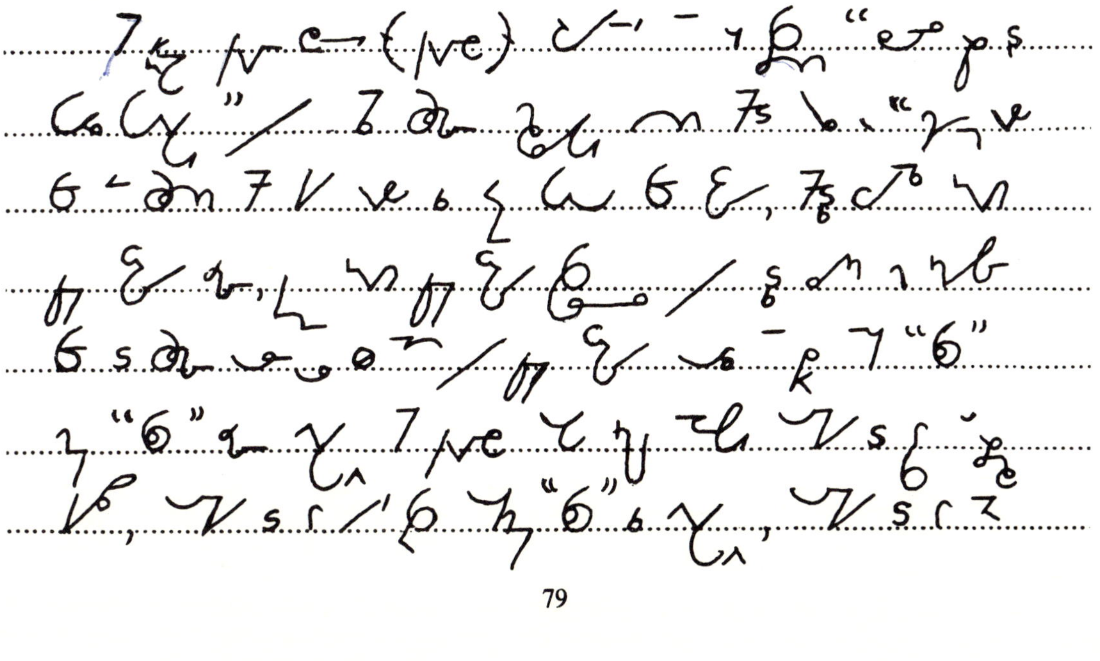

[Shorthand text]

[Teeline shorthand outlines]

SUPPLEMENTARY EXERCISE 23

Read and copy

"Mr" or "Esquire"

[Teeline shorthand outlines]

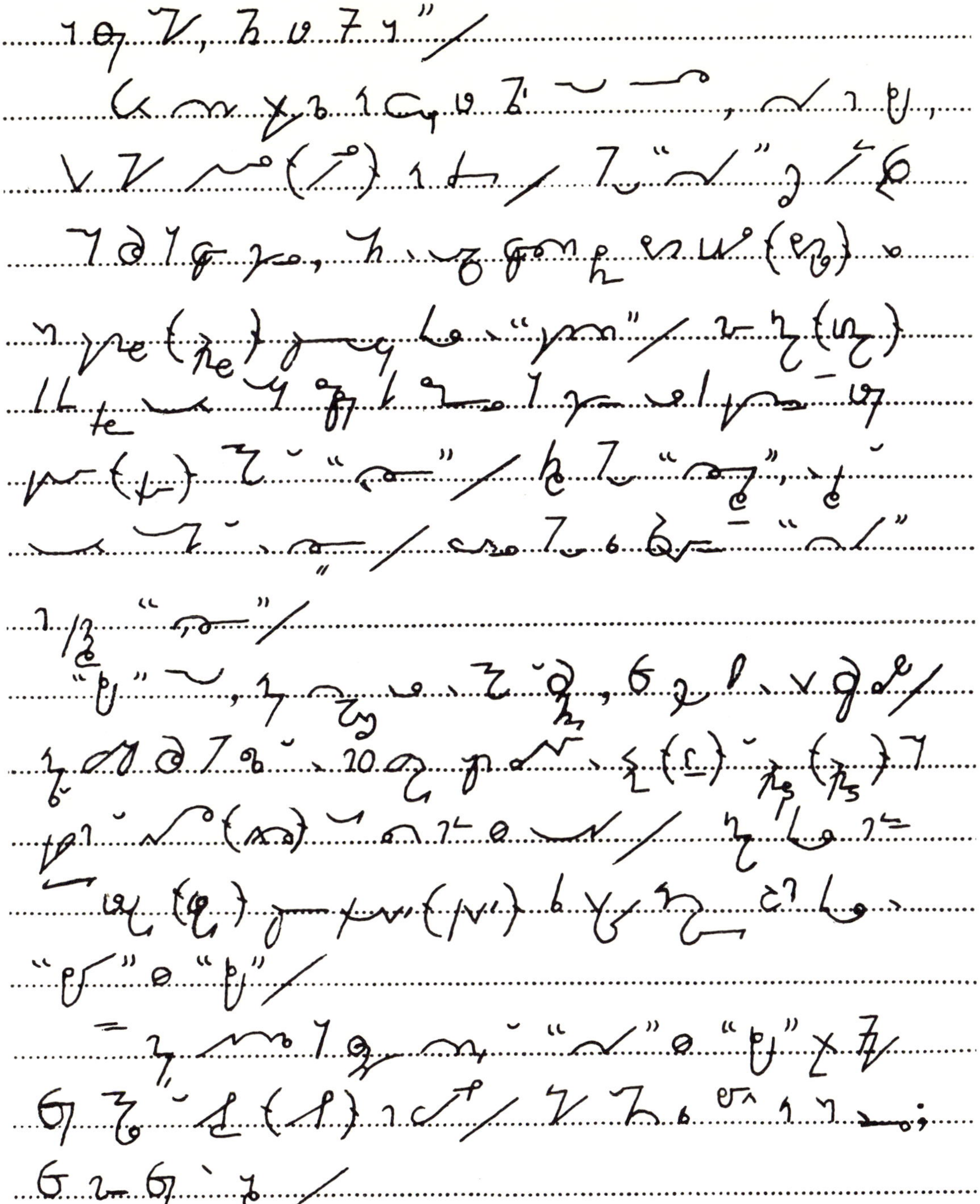

Food

[shorthand content]

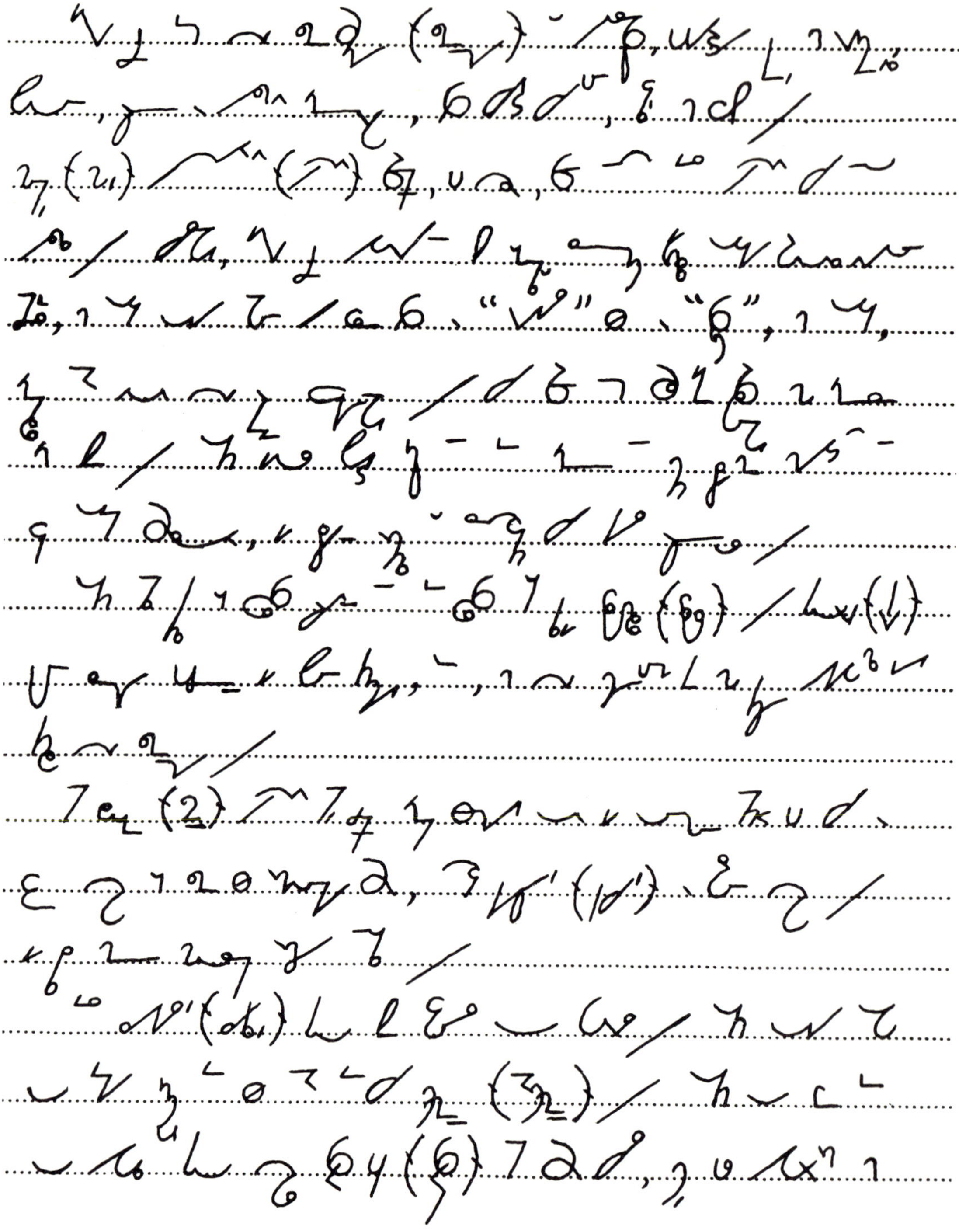

[shorthand notation]

SUPPLEMENTARY EXERCISE 25

Holidays

[shorthand notation]

Keys to exercises

Longhand keys for Teeline exercises are counted and marked every ten words so that they may be used for timed dictation and repetition drills.

Alternatively, the longhand key may be used as a longhand-into-Teeline exercise then checked from the Teeline in the exercise.

* All longhand keys are marked in tens for dictation purposes.

KEY TO EXERCISE 3C

Key to Exercise

1. We are very busy all day, for we have to / go to the office. (14)
2. If we meet Dan today, we shall be happy to / take him with us to the garage. (17)
3. We will fetch the car and then go on to / the coffee bar. (13)
4. We have a new car. It is a yellow one. / Shall we go for a ride in it? (18)
5. I know who has the new lipstick in stock. We / can go to the shop where it is sold while / we are out. (23)
6. Allan is not well. He has had to stay in / bed all day. (13)
7. I am by myself today. Please call and have a / cup of tea with me. (15)
8. The red pills are in the yellow box. The blue / ones are in a parcel in my basket. (18)
9. The letter is dated today. Do you know who wrote / it? (11)
10. I have put some cake in the basket and made / a thermos of coffee, so we can stop for a / snack on the way. (24)

KEY TO EXERCISE 3D

1. Have a cup of this cocoa. It is excellent. Ann / made it. (12)
2. Wipe the cups and plates for me. I am very / busy today and could do with some help. (18)
3. Shall we have some curry for dinner? I have already / cooked the rice, so it will not take much time / to finish it. (23)
4. My coat has faded and as I paid a good / sum for it, I shall take it back to the / shop and see what they say. (26)
5. They say that blue always fades at the seaside. I / shall have to have it dyed. (16)
6. The milk is in the blue jug on the shelf. / Take it into the kitchen for me. (17)

7. For dinner we had roast duck and cabbage, with sago / for sweet and coffee, cheese and biscuits to finish / the meal. (22)
8. I have a date at noon with the girl you / noticed in the shop. (14)
9. He slipped at the quarry and hurt his neck. They / had to carry him home to bed. (17)
10. Can you let me have a copy of the book / on Teeline? I wish to study the new system of / fast writing. (22)

KEY TO EXERCISE 3G

1. The Chairman of the firm said he fully expected to / have some useful information to bring to the notice of / his board by the end of February. (27)
2. The judge quoted the case of a wife who had / been granted half the value of her husband's estate following / an accident which she had survived, but which was due / to a careless error. (34)
3. We shall let you have the goods which you requested / by express delivery in the morning. (16)
4. He needs an x-ray as he has had a cough / for months. They do not seem to know what / is causing it and the medicine he has been taking / does not seem to be doing him any good. I / am sure he will end up in hospital. (48)
5. You should now know your Teeline alphabet, and you will / be surprised how much you are able to write already. / If you had been studying any other system of shorthand / there would be very few things which you could write / by this time. Your vocabulary would be very limited and / you would have lists of special out-lines to memorize which / you would find very tedious. So, make the most of / your good luck and use what you know every time / you have a chance to put it into practice. This / way you will build up a speed right from the / first lesson. (102)

KEY TO EXERCISE 4B

1. We will have dinner at the Hilton Hotel. They keep / a very good cider there. The last time we were / there we had some excellent mutton. (26)
2. I have written to my aunt in London to ask / if I can visit her this summer. She has a / house near Covent Garden Market. (25)
3. Mr. Thornton is the founder of our club. He might / give us a lecture in February. It would be the / best time for a talk. (25)
4. In most cases, children today are not brought up so / strictly as their parents were. (15)
5. A large number of people gathered in the square to / demonstrate their loyalty to the President. (16)
6. This cotton is not quite the right colour. Will it / matter? I have cut out the satin slip and want / to get on with it. The pattern is very easy. / (30)

7. The picture is not level. Can you straighten it for / me? I think it should be lower as well. / I should value your opinion on the matter.   (28)
8. You can learn better if you have a good memory, / but hard work will help you to master any skill.   (20)
9. A verdict of accidental death was recorded by the coroner / at the inquest.   (13)
10. The boy had concussion after his accident in the town / centre, and was in the hospital annexe for fourteen days.   (20)

KEY TO EXERCISE 4F

1. I have signed the letter which we are sending to / Mr. Rudd. It might excite his interest if we were / also to include a picture of the yacht.   (28)
2. The metal parts of the motor scooter were tarnished, and / its paint was badly scratched, so Peter decided not to / buy it.   (23)
3. When we attended matins at Holy Trinity Church, the choir / sang the 'Te Deum' in Latin, and then an extract / was read from the Book 'Exodus' by the rector.   (29)
4. He was annoyed when their quiet tête-a-tête was / rudely interrupted by the waiter bringing the bill, but refrained / from commenting upon the matter.
5. The vintage wine was quite potent. The old workman was / completely knocked out by it that night and was still / feeling dreadful the following morning.   (25)
6. A routine enquiry by the contractor was made on behalf / of the company involved, but they refused to publish their / findings.   (21)
7. The new pavilion will be opened by a war veteran / during Tattoo week, and a speech will be made by / the squadron's padre.   (23)
8. After the volcano erupted there was still more poverty in / the village. Volunteers brought food and medical supplies to help / combat the invading illnesses.   (24)
9. Wanton damage caused by vandals could be reduced in volume / if the general public were more active in spotting and / reporting offenders, instead of turning a blind eye.   (28)

KEY TO EXERCISE 5D

1. I understand the undergraduate's accommodation is extremely uncomfortable and much / too expensive.   (12)
2. Being completely incompatible, they were constantly quarrelling. They must have / been a nuisance to their neighbours in the next flat.   (20)
3. There is an unconfirmed report that she is to be / understudy for the concert pianist. She often accompanies the contralto / we heard last week.   (24)
4. Some people live in a council house for reasons of / economy. Their income is not large enough for them to / consider buying a home of their own.   (27)
5. I feel the comment was not intended to be complimentary, / but I think we should consider the matter further before taking action.   (22)

6. If you intend to transfer these funds, please complete the / enclosed form and retain the counterfoil. (16)
7. In contrast to her sister, she is most self-reliant. / It is hard to convince people that they are related. (20)

KEY TO EXERCISE 5E

(Reading exercise)

1. She is an accomplished writer, who has composed many / songs as well as producing books. (16)
2. Nothing is more likely to cause irritation than constant banging / when a person is trying to rest. (17)
3. Old people need to be protected from many things, and / need extra consideration even if they are irritating at times. / (20)
4. I have lost my bangle. Have you seen it? No, / but there are two rings lying on the sideboard. (19)
5. I am longing for a day in the country, but / I have not been able to get away from the / business for several weeks. (24)
6. We have no hesitation in strongly recommending this newspaper for / its general knowledge content. (14)
7. In business and trade, capital plays an important part. In / addition, enterprise is necessary. (14)
8. It is our concern that they should not be exposed / to further irritation in connection with this matter. (18)
9. It seems a long time since we went off on / an expedition and got some fresh air into our lungs. (20)
10. The bank's recommendation will strengthen our chances of being given / the contract. (12)

KEY TO EXERCISE 5F

1. Your bank will advise you how to arrange payment for / this consignment. (12)
2. I agree that she is more self-willed than her / brother, but she has a number of accomplishments which compel / my admiration. (22)
3. In this uncommon situation we strongly advise the immediate payment / of the supplementary allowances. (14)
4. I should like you to accompany me to the bank. / I need some information on the exchange position, before I / decide what to do regarding my investments. (27)
5. The biologist, though capable, was temperamental, and was frequently in / trouble with his colleagues on this account. (17)
6. His cheerfulness and the nobility of his character showed themselves / in his photograph, although it was not a specially good / likeness in other ways. (24)
7. As we looked seaward, the hopelessness of our situation became / horribly clear to us. We tried to be sensible and / to remain calm. (23)

8. It was laughable to see the fatuousness of their expressions / as they queued for the pop star's autograph. (18)
9. After the controversial report was handed round for the committee / to see, the Chairman had to bang on the table / to restore order to the meeting. (26)
10. Our programme of educational topics for the coming season covers / a wide range of subjects, from archaeology to zoology. (19)

KEY TO EXERCISE 6A

(1) *enter, inter, etc.* I hesitate to interfere with the arrangements but I must / [10] point out that to introduce a visitor such as Mr. / [20] Brown at that stage of the entertainment would not be / [30] at all suitable. It would appear to me that it / [40] would be far better to introduce him at a later / [50] stage, for example, some time during the second part of / [60] the proceedings when people will be far more receptive to / [70] a speech such as he will give. (77)

(2) An important element in our lives today is entertainment, whether / [10] by means of the cinema, theatre or television. We live / [20] today at a far greater pace than people used to / [30] do so we must interpose some form of relaxation into / [40] our work. Without such an intermission we would not get / [50] very far, but we must always take care that the / [60] introduction of entertainment does not interfere with our work. (69)

(3) *under* It must be understood that in undertaking this mission, we / [10] the undersigned, want nothing introducing into this appeal for charity, / [20] which would suggest that we view a certain section of / [30] the public as underdogs, who are to be treated as / [40] though they have no opinions of their own. This is / [50] no underground movement, and we must make sure that is / [60] thoroughly understood. It may have been so in the past, / [70] but we have all undergone a change since those days. / [80] (80)

(4) *trans* It transpired that the transaction was undertaken with the best / [10] intentions, but during the transitory period it was decided to / [20] transfer some of the cargo to another shipping line. When / [30] this became known, the company would not entertain the idea / [40] any further, and the deal fell through. It was felt / [50] that to undertake such a transfer was contrary to the / [60] best interests of the transaction and would interfere with the / [70] plans which had been made. We now understand that the / [80] transaction may be considered again in a few months time / [90] and this view has been transmitted to those concerned. (99)

7

(5) *auto*   This new automobile has an automatic transmission system and the / whole ¹⁰

arrangement is so elementary in concept that it can / be readily understood by the ²⁰

most simple person. In addition, / the motor is so arranged that no problems of ³⁰

maintenance / are introduced, and we understand that it compares very favourably / ⁴⁰ ⁵⁰

with more orthodox methods of transport.   (56)

(6) *Word endings*

  (a) Whether we go eastward, westward, northward, or southward, we shall eventually
      come to the sea.
  (b) A record player used to be called a gramophone, before that it was called a phono-
      graph.
  (c) It is now very expensive to send a telegram. The telephone is quicker and cheaper.
  (d) The psychologist is a very sensible man who will help any person in trouble. He
      is writing for a new controversial magazine which will be published shortly.
  (e) The noise was so great it was impossible for them to hear themselves speak.
  (f) We should congratulate ourselves on reaching a satisfactory solution to the problem.
  (g) I am very partial to doing crossword puzzles, but some people are not able to find
      enjoyment in this way.

KEY TO EXERCISE 6B

1. A spokesman for the Council said the matter was not / their concern, but they ¹⁰

    might consider it. Their income was / not as considerable as some people imagined. ²⁰

    They tried to / make the best possible use of their resources, but they / could not ³⁰ ⁴⁰

    accomplish everything desired of them without time to / study all aspects of the sit- ⁵⁰

    uation. In the present state / of the country's economy, he doubted whether this ⁶⁰

    was the / right time to plan such improvements as those suggested.   (79) ⁷⁰

2. In reply to questions, the policeman said he had merely / asked the young man to ¹⁰

    accompany him to the police / station and to make a statement. The prisoner had ²⁰

    then / attacked him. Counsel for the Defence tried to prove that / the blow had ³⁰ ⁴⁰

    been struck in self-defence. Summing up, the / judge congratulated the policeman ⁵⁰

    on his self-control in a trying / situation. They could not tolerate such attacks on ⁶⁰

    the police, / who were acting in the interests of the general public. /   (80) ⁷⁰ ⁸⁰

3. The retiring President was presented with a gold watch at / the Annual General
Meeting last night. Mr. Freeman, who made / the presentation on behalf of the
members, said that Mr. / Green had been instrumental in bringing the Club into
being / and they were sorry that for personal reasons connected with / his health,
it was now necessary for them to elect / a new President. He had no doubt that from
time / to time, they would see Mr. Green in a social capacity, / and he wished him
a long and happy retirement. (89)

4. From the fragmentary evidence before us we would say the / conclusions are not
as obvious as the speaker would have / us believe. The whole thing is still at an
experimental / stage and there are many supplementary questions which arise. There /
is, for instance, the problem of manufacturing on a sufficiently / large scale to
make the venture into an economical proposition. / (60)

KEY TO EXERCISE 7A

1. Thank you for your letter of the 5th, and for / your order for 2½ tons of
domestic fuel. (20)
2. During the year, our output has exceeded five hundred thousand / tons,
which is 3¼ times as much as / it was two years ago. (24)
3. Shall we turn over to electricity this year, or would / you prefer to retain the
coal fires? If the latter, we / shall need to order 1¾ tons of / coal while we can
get it at the summer price. / (40)
4. They guarantee to let us have two-thirds of our order / before the end of
next week and the remainder by / the end of the month. (25)
5. For seven months now the visible trade deficit has been / running at an
annual rate of £850 million. / (20)
6. By 1971 there will be an unemployment figure / of about one hundred-
thousand out of a working population / of nearly seven hundred thousand. (25)
7. The initial management charge on capital invested is only / 3¾ per cent, out
of which 1¼ / per cent is paid out in commission on orders. (29)
8. The Company's funds already stand at over six million, one / hundred and
thirty thousand pounds and the offer price of / the units has risen by 35⅓
per cent. (30)

KEY TO EXERCISE 8A

pale pail Paul pal pool leek leak bet beet beat like lick cote cot coat mull mule
bought boot cool coal peg pig wreck rock reek rick rack guest gust ghost
square squire this these those thus chose choose week weak wick Wyke lead led
load volume velum swop swoop sweep peace piece poem deity via Iona Moira
adapt adopt. (60)

91

KEY TO EXERCISE 9A

1. British Rail and British Road Services have had to face / many a crisis. (13)
2. Credit sales in these days form a large part of / the retail trade. (13)
3. We often grumble, but rarely take steps to alter what / we grumble about. (13)
4. In reply to their enquiry, the secretary produced excellent references. (10)
5. If they do not comply with the regulations, we shall / be compelled to take legal action. (16)
6. The Archbishop promised to arrange for a member of the / monastic order to be interviewed for the television programme. (19)
7. Doris has made a satin dress. It is ever so / pretty, but her brother does not like it. (18)
8. They expect to visit Europe during this year. I hope / they will have fine weather for their trip. (18)
9. An orange, eaten before breakfast, makes a better start to / the day than a cup of tea. (17)
10. The ground in this garden is barren. The soil is / too dry for most plants to grow well. However, we / have ample space in the greenhouse to supply most of / our needs. (32)
11. To make a quick after-dinner sweet, break some bread into / crumbs and fry until crisp. Put between layers of stewed / fruit and chill in the 'fridge. Serve with fresh cream. / (30)
12. Some people adopt a simple approach to things because they / find it gives them ample opportunity to ask supplementary questions. / (20)
13. We must do all we can to protect these people, / but it will be necessary to prod them into activity / for their own sake, otherwise their position will be very awkward. / (30)
14. In spite of the great rise in the cost of / our raw materials, we have been able to increase production / sufficiently to produce a profit over the year. (28)
15. Your studies will soon be complete and with sufficient practice / you will become an accomplished writer of Teeline. (18)
16. Dear Sir, We thank you for your letter of the / 24th and, as requested, enclose a copy of the catalogue / you need. We also enclose a receipt for the cheque / sent with your letter.
Yours faithfully, (36)

KEY TO EXERCISE 9B

1. The speaker made a number of complimentary remarks about the / position which the firm had adopted in the matter. They / had approached the experiment with open minds, and had given / their research staff all the co-operation they required in the / way of time, money and equipment. He thought this was / the right attitude for the leaders of industry to adopt / at the present time, and the results had fully justified / their far-sightedness. (72)

2. Centuries ago, people used to keep a "commonplace book" into / which they copied extracts which appealed to them. It was / also the custom to keep diaries, and the writing of / long letters in beautiful handwriting was considered to be a / duty one had to one's friends. Today, life is not / so simple as that, and we have no time for / making extracts, keeping diaries or writing long letters. What do / we do with our time, which will be of interest / to future generations? (83)

3. Gentlemen,
   In reply to your letter of yesterday, we regret / to inform you that we cannot agree with you over / the question of payment for our last consignment of goods. /
   The quality of this delivery was well below that of / the sample from which we ordered, and we feel, in / the circumstances, that you should either offer us the goods / at a reduced cost, or replace them.
   We await a / further communication from you on the matter.
                                        Yours truly,   (79)

93

4. Dear Sirs,

We are pleased to know that you were / satisfied with the material we sent you last week, and / thank you for your repeat order. Unfortunately, owing to delay / in receiving our supplies of raw materials, we are at / the moment entirely out of stock of this material and / it will be at least two weeks before we can / meet your demands.

However, we enclose samples and particulars of / material of a similar quality, which we have in stock / in case you can make use of this immediately.

Assuring / you of our prompt attention at all times.

We are, / Yours faithfully, (102)

KEY TO EXERCISE 9C

1. Dear Sir,

We are taking the liberty of sending you / with this letter, a copy of our new catalogue and / price-list.

We are an old-established firm who can / supply you with first-class stock at realistic prices. In / addition, we offer discount for cash.

If you are interested / in dealing with us, we should be pleased to send / one of our representatives to call upon you. Just write / or telephone us at the address given above.

Yours faithfully, / (80)

2. The Chairman in the course of his speech, said that / during the year under review, profits had risen by six / per cent. This was in spite of having borne the / cost of new plant and machinery in three factories and / losses sustained on account of the dock strike in the / early part of the year.

On the foreign side, turnover / had increased considerably and there was every indication that it / would be even greater in volume in the coming year. / (80)

3. We regret to state that our sales in the United / States for the year ending December 1967 were rather lower / than we expected, and as you will see in the / Directors' Report it has been decided to declare a dividend / of only 3%. Furthermore, I am instructed to / inform you that additional expenses are expected in the United / Kingdom between now and next April, and your Board of / Directors appeal to you to do everything possible to increase / output and cut production costs. (85)

4. Dear Sir,

In reply to your letter of last Wednesday, / we are sending you, under separate cover, our latest catalogue / and price list. As you will see, we offer discount / for cash.

We hope to receive your order at your / earliest convenience and take this opportunity of assuring you of / our best attention at all times.

Yours truly, (58)

KEY TO SUPPLEMENTARY EXERCISE 1

1. add added Adam about abbey Bob baby bed beads barring bored bus busy cabs cuffs coughing

2. cake case caused cats dab daubing did deeds deaf does date dog dove dart end ended

3. eggs face facing figs foggy fake phase fast facet good gales games gone gave garb

4. guard girl his hair hurry hired hemmed hill holly hack in ink imp ill jade jugs

5. joke joking jam keg killing keel keen lice like looking log lambs leaning lined lanes mob made

6. maids mug mare mean many knobs kneel names near nearly odd oats open piece

7. paid pages pegged pin pairs parrot paired quit quote queer rib robbed Robert rabbit real

8. rally rain rent rose rave write red sob sobs socks six safe seller seems soon soap stop

9. stem stag stake stiff slipped slipper stove stow share spilled spanner scared tabs toad

10. tidy dough tug tugged Teeline test vice vague veal vain vanes view velvet valid

11. web wed wedding walking wall will woman when weep wipe weave

12. woven excel excellent expose exam yolk yell yelled yams bat batted cost coated coded

13. cadet loaded fated faded quoted state exported expired host post posted teaser restive request

14. requested case sag guest loss last sons sums busy babies daisy desired dispose mason boss bosses

15. doses bast Feb. fable fellow for forget ferry few fix shelf muff puff wife

KEY TO SUPPLEMENTARY EXERCISE 2

KEY TO SUPPLEMENTARY EXERCISE 3

(1)

(2)

(3)

(4)

(5)

(6)

(7)

(8)

(9)

(10)

KEY TO SUPPLEMENTARY EXERCISE 4

(1)
(2)
(3)

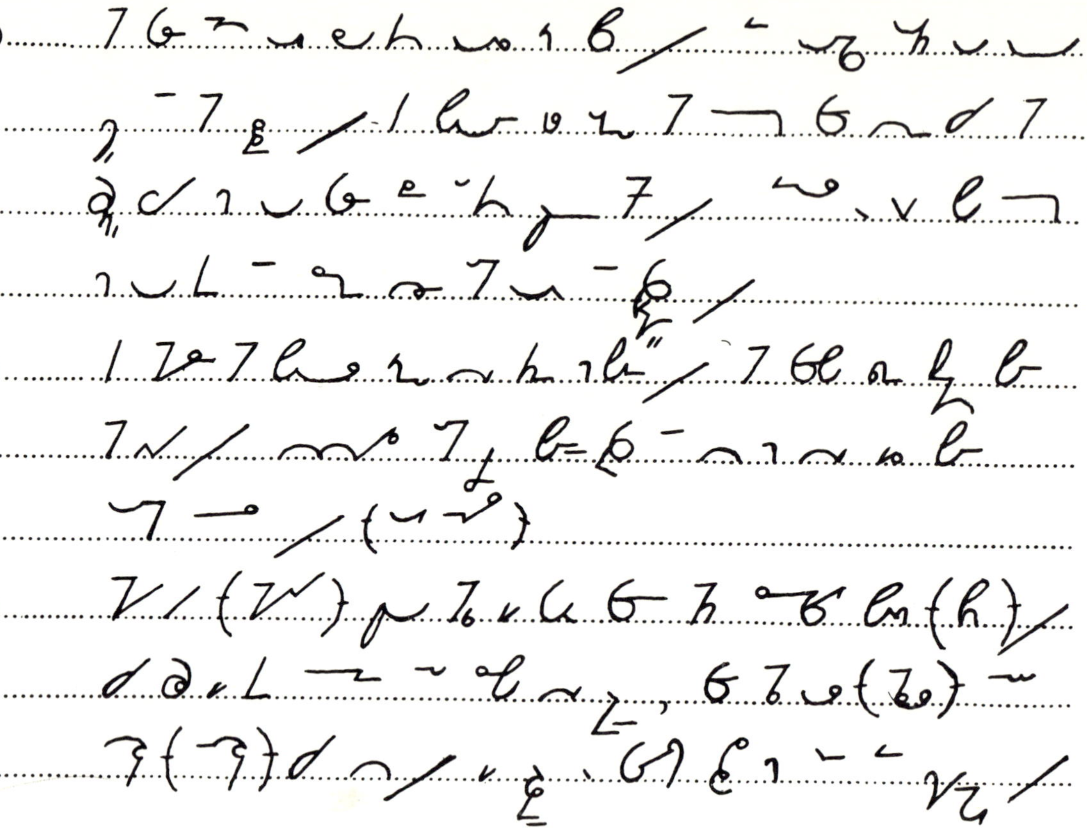

KEY TO SUPPLEMENTARY EXERCISE 5

(1)
(2)
(3)
(4)
(5)

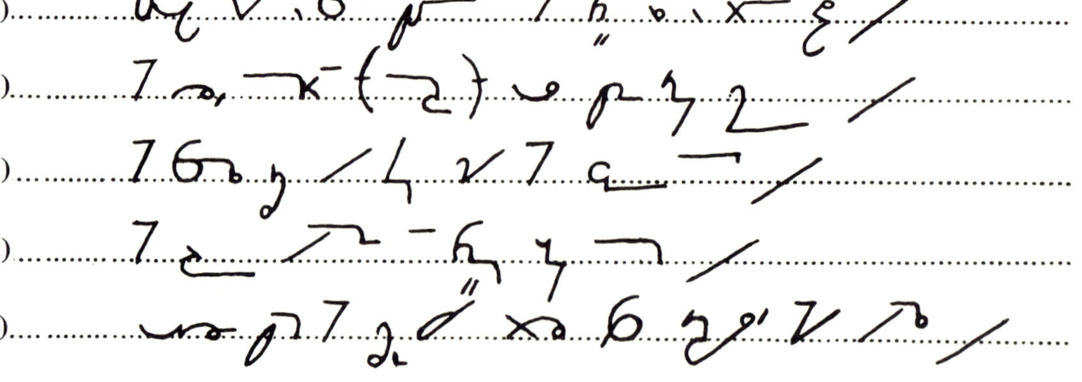

(6)

(7)

(8)

(9)

(10)

KEY TO SUPPLEMENTARY EXERCISE 6

(1)

(2)

(3)

(4)

(5)

(6)

(7)

(8)

(9)

(10)

KEY TO SUPPLEMENTARY EXERCISE 7

(1) (2) (3) (4) (5)

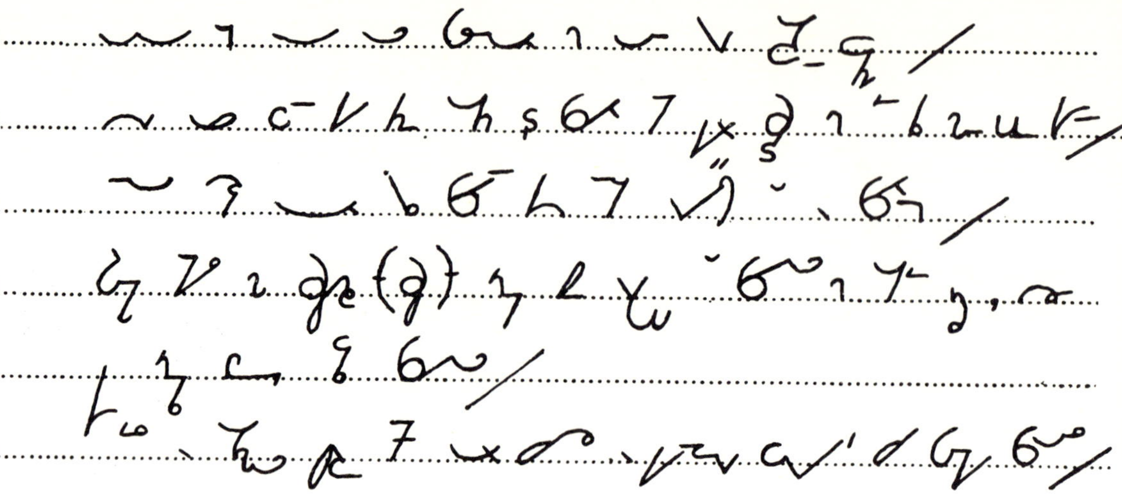

KEY TO SUPPLEMENTARY EXERCISE 8

(1) (2) (3) (4) (5) (6)

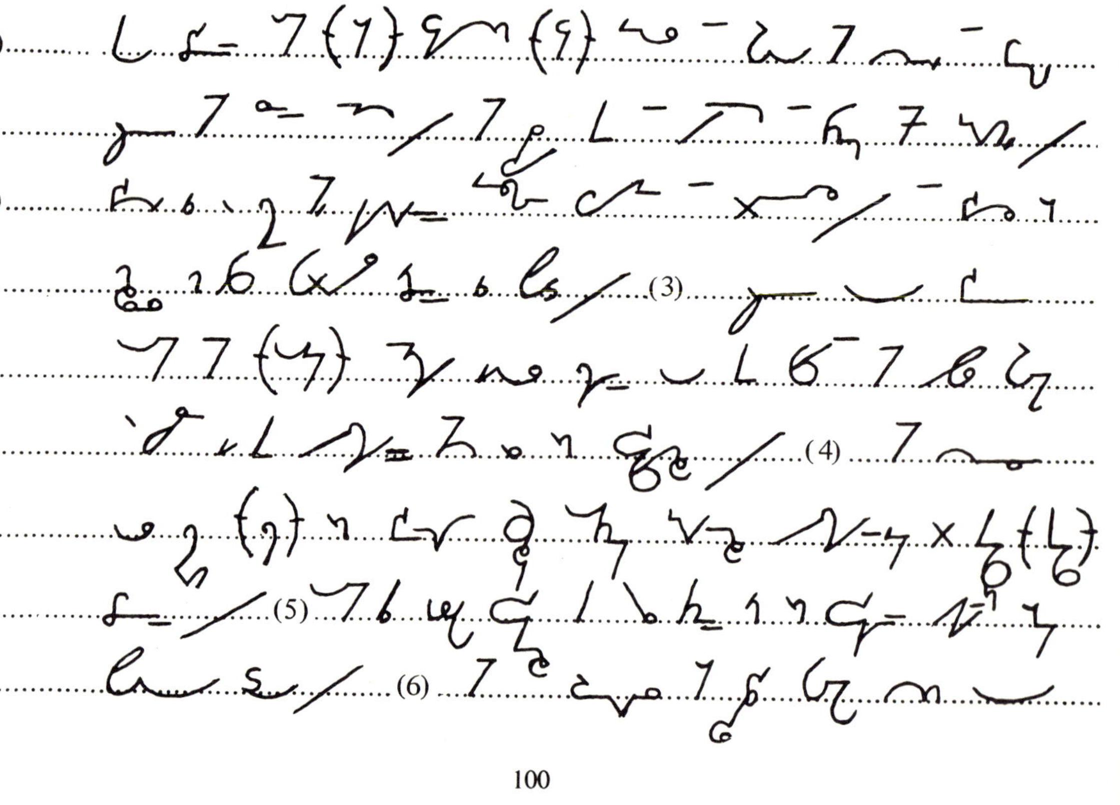

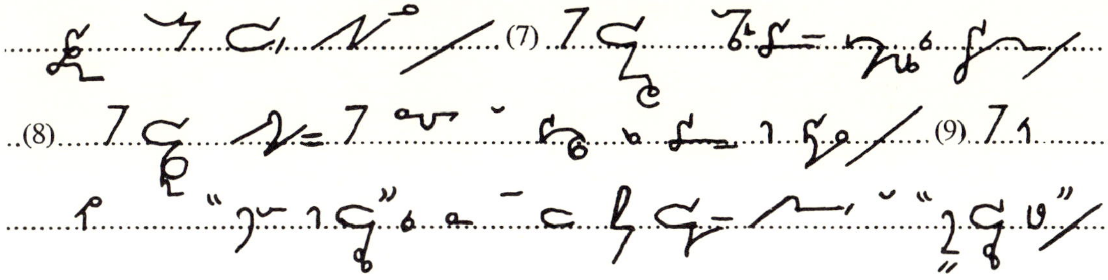

KEY TO SUPPLEMENTARY EXERCISE 9

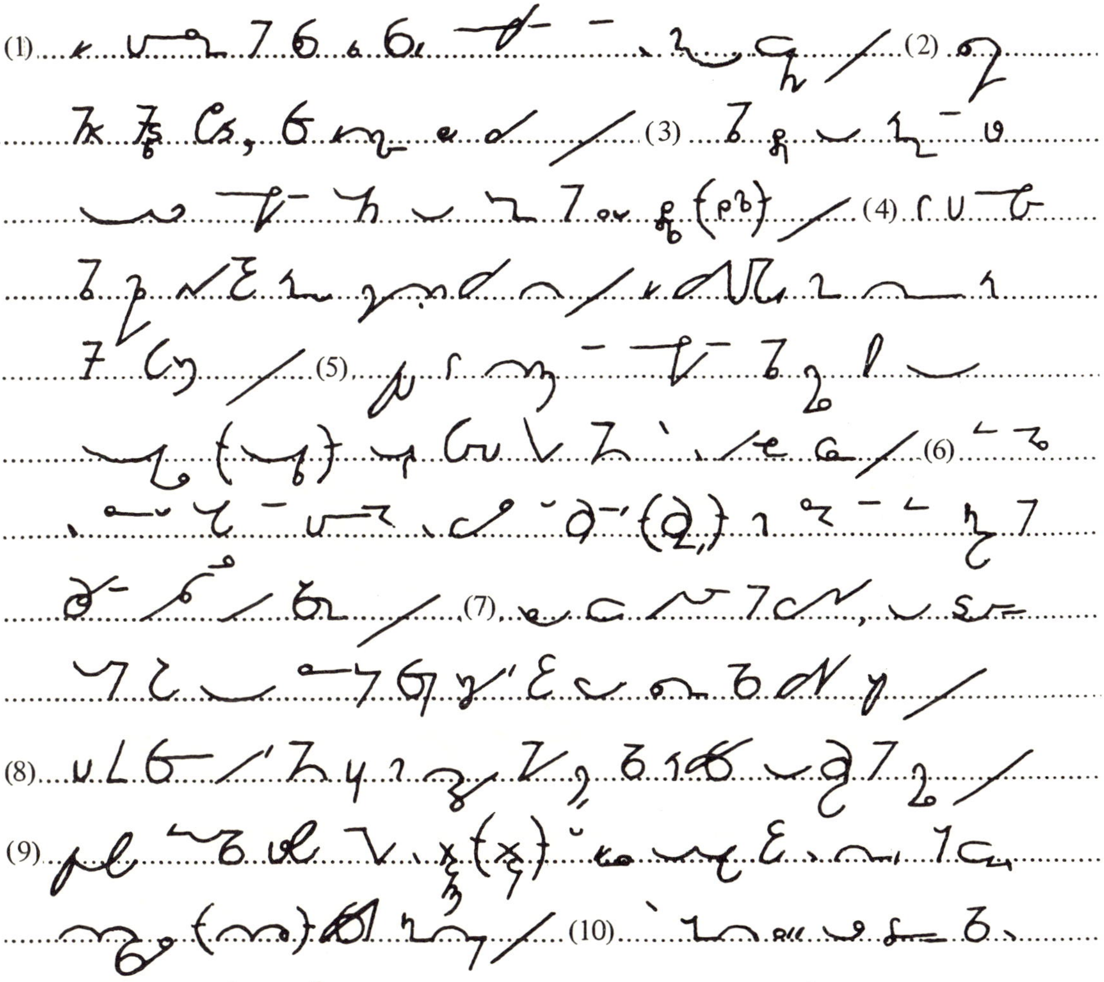

KEY TO SUPPLEMENTARY EXERCISE 10

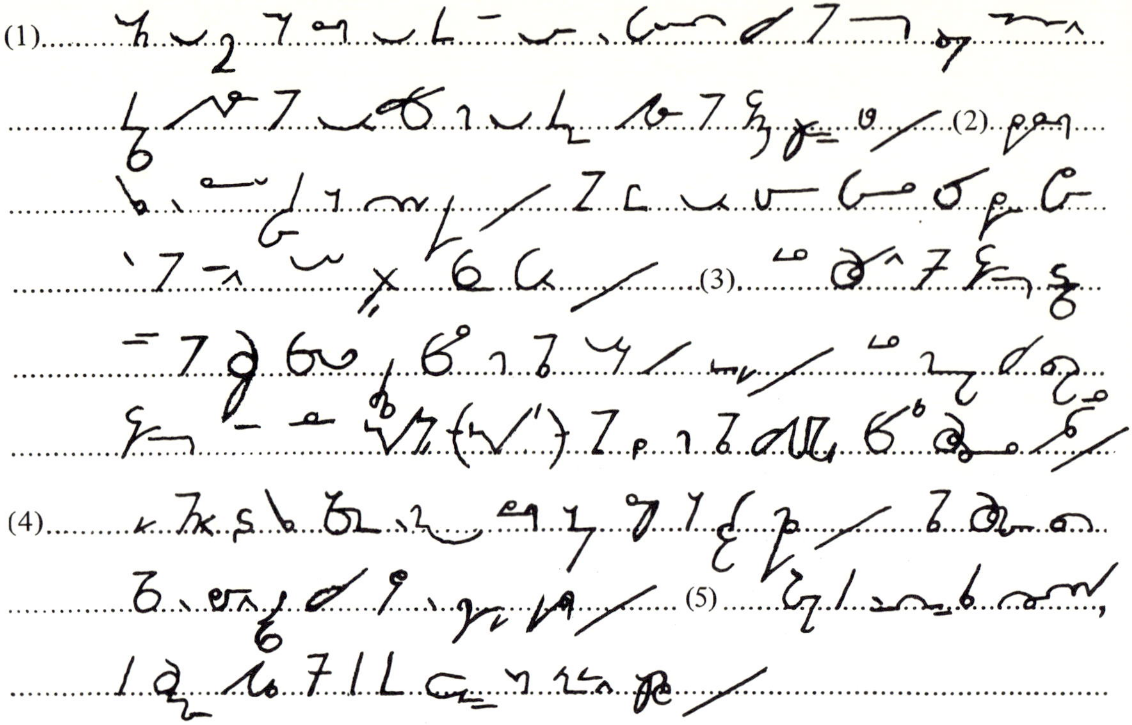

KEY TO SUPPLEMENTARY EXERCISE 11

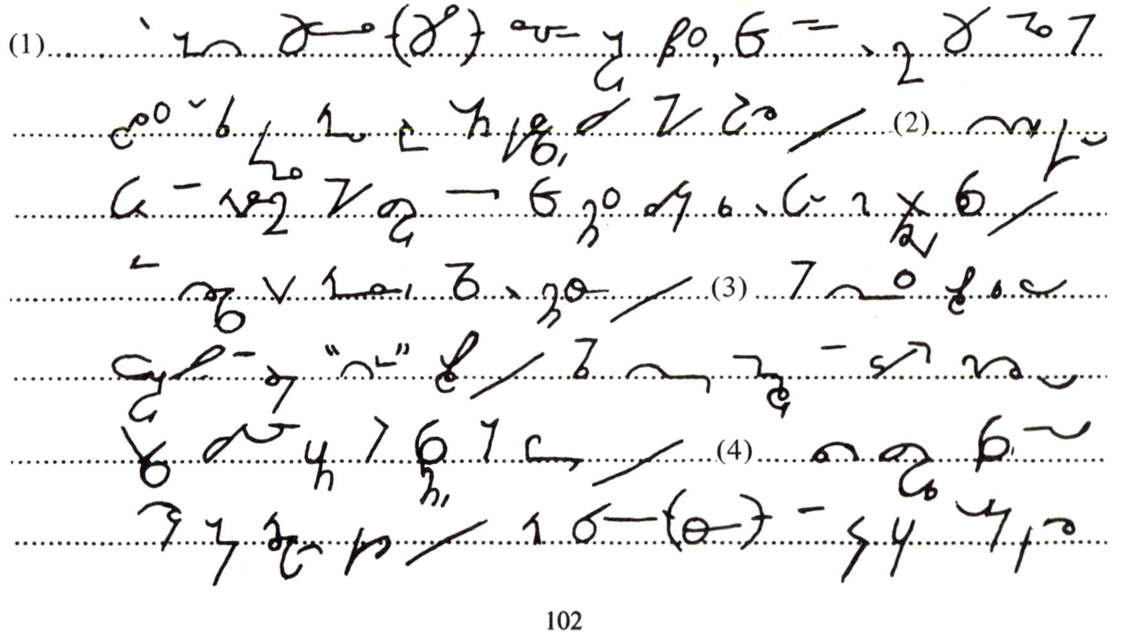

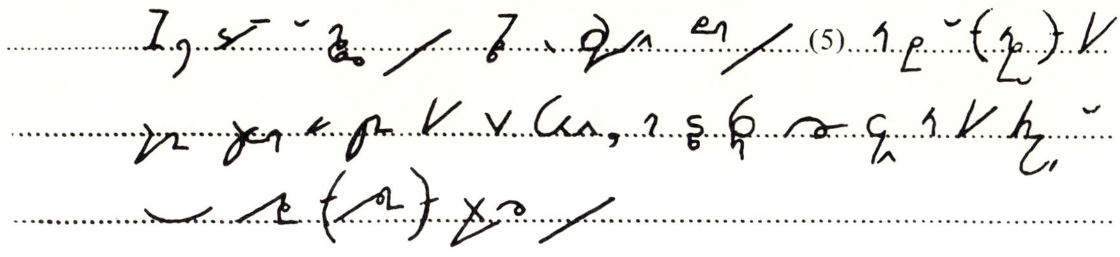

KEY TO SUPPLEMENTARY EXERCISE 12

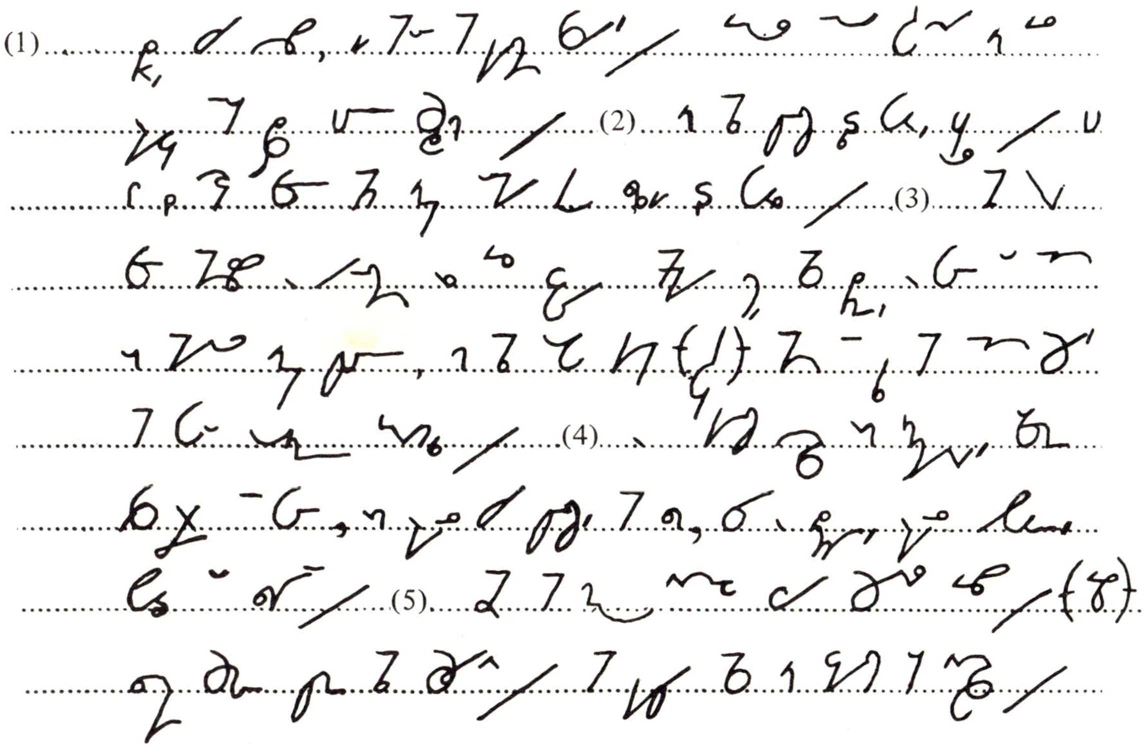

KEY TO SUPPLEMENTARY EXERCISE 13

(a) Time is something about which everyone has thought at some / time, but we rarely think very deeply about its nature. / We speak of saving time, being short of time, making / time, wasting time, and killing time. There are even many / people to whom 'Big Time' and 'Small Time' mean something. /

When we are not making progress, we say we are / marking time, and the elderly man or woman often says, / 'In my time we made better use of our time / when we were not working, but in those days there / was not much time we could call our own.'   *(99 words)*

(b) This is the time of the year when those of us / who enjoy gardening anxiously watch the weather. The instructions / on the colourful packets which contain our seeds - and our / hopes - tell us to sow the seeds during March or / April, 'when the ground is in proper condition'.

Sometimes it / seems to me that every time I feel like sowing / my seeds the ground is too wet or has not / that 'fine tilth' my gardening book demands. Day after wet / or windy day goes by and suddenly, I realise that / it is too late: I must go and buy plants / as usual.   *(102 words)*

KEY TO SUPPLEMENTARY EXERCISE 14

(a)

(b)

(c)

(d)

8

[Teeline shorthand content]

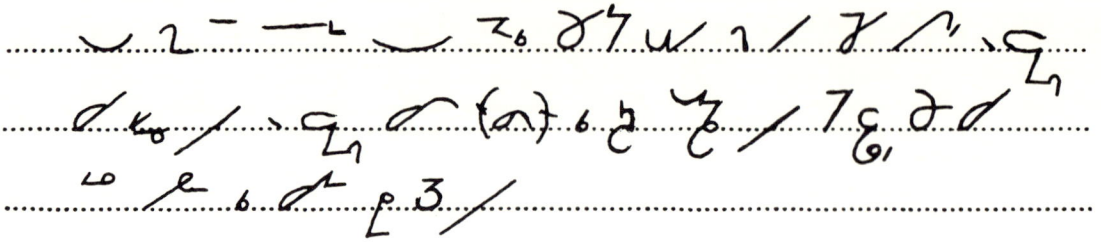

KEY TO SUPPLEMENTARY READING EXERCISES 21

A. Nottingham Goose Fair is said to be the oldest Fair / in the country. It takes place on the first Thursday, / Friday, and Saturday in October on an open space called / 'The Forest' not far from the city centre. At noon / on Thursday, the Lord Mayor opens the Fair by ringing / a bell. He is usually attended by other noted citizens / including the Sheriff of Nottingham.

The local school children are / granted a whole day's holiday on the Friday. Why this / has come about no-one seems to know, as Saturday / afternoon is generally considered to be the children's time.

Traditional / sweetmeats at Fair time are brandy snaps and Grantham ginger-bread / which may be found on sale at most local shops / and which then seem to disappear until the following October. /

No geese are sold nowadays, but the human variety flock / nightly to the Fairground ready and willing to be 'plucked'. *(150 words)*

B. In the traditional British song 'Rule Britannia' we hear the / words 'Britons never shall be slaves'. Slaves of what? There / are other ways of being a slave than by being ruled / by a member of a conquering race. For instance, my / neighbours are slaves to their motorcars. Every spare moment is / spent in vehicle worship. They do not own their cars; / they are owned by them.

Some people are slaves to / football, others to the smoking habit, some women are slaves / to their families or their homes.

It is not necessarily / a bad thing to be in bondage to something or / someone, but it is perhaps important for us to / think carefully before we allow ourselves to fall into slavery. *(120 words)*

The Private Secretary (2)

The ideal private secretary, according to one businessman, 'sounds as / [10] if she looks lovely'. This does not necessarily mean that / [20] she has a 'golden voice', but it does mean that / [30] her voice is kept low but clear, that she is / [40] courteous even if the caller is not, patient even if / [50] the caller blusters. She is serene and unruffled, but she / [60] does not waste words or time. If the caller wishes / [70] to speak to the 'boss' and the 'boss' is not / [80] available, the private secretary will enquire tactfully whether she can / [90] be of assistance herself, whether she can ring back when / [100] the boss is available, whether she can take a message. / [110] If the caller is unknown to her she will ask / [120] for and make a careful note of his or her / [130] name and telephone number. In any case, before putting the / [140] call through to her principal she will tell him who / [150] is ringing and ask him whether he can receive the / [160] call.

The good private secretary does not normally use the / [170] office telephone for private calls particularly during office hours. She / [180] remembers that the firm buys her time during office hours. / [190] Telephone calls, also, are not free, and form a kind / [200] of expense which should not be taken for granted as / [210] a 'fringe benefit'. Incoming calls of course are not chargeable / [220] to the firm, but the employee's time certainly is, and / [230] friends should be discouraged from making personal calls during office / [240] hours.   (241)

'Mr' or 'Esquire'?

'Can you tell me' said Mary, my office junior, 'when / [10] I should use "Esq." and when "Mr"? Some people tell / [20] me always to use "Esq." then somebody else tells me / [30] to use that only for professional people, and sometimes I / [40] don't even know what sort of person I am sending / [50] the letter to. Does it really matter? It is so / [60] confusing.'

'Well Mary' I said, 'there is no need to / [70] be confused. All you have to remember is that it / [80] doesn't really matter at all which you use, but if / [90] your boss prefers one or the other, then use that / [100] one.'

Like many expressions in common use, these two terms, Mr. / [110] and Esq., have their roots in history. The word 'Mr' / [120] goes right back to the days of the craft guilds, / [130] when a would-be craftsman spent seven years as an apprentice, / [140] after which he was a 'journeyman'. Not until he / [150] had produced work which satisfied the high standards of the / [160] guild was he permitted to use the proud title of / 'Master'. Hence the word 'masterpiece', a piece of work worthy / of a Master. Nowadays the word is abbreviated to 'Mr' / and pronounced 'mister'.

'Esquire' too in the middle-ages was a / title of dignity, but grew from a very different / source. In those far-off days the sons of a noble / family often served a kind of apprenticeship to the profession / of arms with some knight or warrior. Until he was / knighted - usually after proving his valour in military action - he / was a 'squire' or 'esquire'.

Today nothing remains of the / original meaning of 'Mr' or 'Esq.' except that they are / both titles of respect and courtesy. Either of them is / suitable in an address; but not both at once! (289)

KEY TO SUPPLEMENTARY READING EXERCISE 24

I have just eaten my Sunday dinner of roast beef / Yorkshire pudding and vegetables, followed, after a reasonable interval, by / fresh fruit, cheese and coffee. Nothing remarkable about that, you / may say; but to me it is remarkable for two / reasons. Firstly, I have just recovered from one of those / strange illnesses which are always around these days, and which / we are told are caused by a 'virus' or a / 'bug', and which, in this case took away my appetite / completely. For about ten days, I had absolutely no interest / in food. When I was foolish enough to eat in / order to gain sufficient nourishment to cope with the day's / work, I suffered agonies of stomach pain for hours afterwards. /

When this happens one becomes afraid to eat, because of / the possible consequences. However, quite suddenly yesterday, I felt hungry, / ate, and my gluttony had no painful repercussions - hence my / Sunday dinner.

The second remarkable thing is that in the / ordinary way I would not thank you for a cooked / meal on Sunday, or any other day, much preferring a / salad meal. I suppose Nature knows the answer to this. /

It is surprising how food colours our lives. When we / are well we either enjoy it or take it for / granted. When we cannot eat we realise how meals break up / the day for us, giving us relaxation and pleasure / as well as sustenance. Without these breaks, the day stretches / emptily before us. Worse still, if one has to prepare / meals for the family, the interest in shopping for and / preparing a good meal departs and the jobs become boring / and irritating chores. When I am not hungry myself I / cannot cook well, so naturally, my husband is as pleased / as I am that my appetite has returned. *(298 words)*

KEY TO SUPPLEMENTARY EXERCISE 25

Immediately after Christmas, every newspaper and magazine will be trying / to tempt me to spend my summer holiday in a / variety of places. According to these advertisements, each place will / be full of sunshine and enchantment. Why is it that / I never respond? I am reminded of an occasion many / years ago, when a party of us were travelling by / road and passed a garden full of dahlias in full / bloom. The beauty of their massed colour drew admiring comments / from us, all except one, who said 'They'll be full / of earwigs'. At the time, we deplored this cynical approach / to life, but I realise that this is my attitude / to holiday advertisements.

One friend who recently spent a month / in a romantic island had to spend most of her / meagre travel allowance on drinking water. In order to enjoy / the sea and sand it was necessary to get up / and out at dawn. Later in the day, the sand / burned the feet and one had to stay indoors out / of the heat.

Another who took a cruise, found it / impossible to sleep at night because of the noise of / generating machinery on the boat. Consequently, in two weeks she / returned, a nervous wreck!

When one is young, travel is / an adventure. The discomforts, the dangers, the inconveniences, are all / part of the holiday - something to talk about when one / returns.

I think I have reached the age where comfort / counts for more than adventure, and when like Kipling's cat, / 'All places are alike to me!' Maybe, if one did / not have to make up one's mind at least six / months beforehand, I would decide on a fine sunny morning / to try one of these wonderful holidays. But as it / is I expect in the end, I shall stay at / home. There I am sure of peace, comfort, good food / and the opportunity to do as I like. I suppose, / that is really all one requires for a holiday and / it is certainly cheaper than going away.

However, I do / hope the advertisements continue. I get such pleasure from reading / them!

(351 words)

Specimen examination papers

(By kind permission of The East Midland Educational Union)

40 words per minute: (5 minutes):

Dear Sir or Madam,

It is with great pleasure that / we announce the opening of our new pets' home. It / has always been difficult to find a suitable place to / leave your cat or dog while you go away on / holiday. It has often been necessary to send them many / miles to a strange town. Now that we have opened / our new home, all that is past. You can leave / your pet with us only an hour or so before / you leave on your holiday and you can pick him / up again on your way home.

If your dog or / cat requires special food, we will make sure that he / gets it for all the time that you are away. / If he becomes ill, he will receive the best care / it is possible to obtain. You can go away in / the sure knowledge that your pet is in good hands / and is enjoying his holiday as much as you are. /

We feel sure that you will agree that our charges / are very moderate after you have read the enclosed price / list.

If you require our services just phone us and / we will collect your pet immediately,

We are,

Yours faithfully, (200)

50 words per minute: (5 minutes):

Gentlemen,

We were very pleased to receive your instructions to / advise your committee as to the best ways of heating / your village hall. We sent a team of our experts / to look over your hall and the following is a / short summary of their report.

110

The present system of heating / is very old and must cost a great deal to / run. It is recommended that the present system should be / replaced by a completely new one as this would prove / to be much cheaper in the long run and would / cost much less to operate.

Electric heating is very easy / to install and has the advantage of being very clean. / Several different methods can be used. One system stores up / the heat during the night when the charge for electricity / is much less. Instant heat can be provided by fan / heaters, but they are a little noisy. The cost for / electricity would work out to about two shillings and sixpence / an hour.

Gas is not available in your village, unless / gas which is stored in a drum is used. Oil / heating is very efficient but is rather costly to install. / A good deal of work would have to be done / in the hall if this system were used. It is / cheaper to run than electricity, costing about two shillings for / each hour.

Please study the enclosed details carefully and let / us know as soon as possible when your committee reach / a decision. The work will take four weeks.

Yours faithfully, (250)

60 words per minute: (5 minutes):

Dear Madam,
    Thank you for your letter of last week / and for your request for details of our wools and / knitted goods. We enclose a card giving full particulars and / samples of the wools we supply. You will see that / we stock a full range of colours in all types / from two-ply to quick-knit.

Since we sell direct / from our own mills, we are able to offer you / this wool at a price much less than you could / buy it in the shops. On orders amounting to over / thirty shillings we also allow a discount of one shilling / and sixpence in the pound. In addition, postage will be / paid by us on all orders.

The enclosed leaflet shows / a selection of our twin sets and sweaters. These articles / combine first-class design with one hundred per cent pure / soft wool. They are a joy to wear, and as / you can see, the prices are most reasonable in relation / to the quality.

As you are a new customer, we / have pleasure in enclosing a voucher worth ten shillings to / post with your order. This is not valid after the / thirty-first of August. It can be used only to / purchase the knitted goods. The leaflet, of course, cannot show / you the lovely shades, but we do have a catalogue / available in full colour, which may be obtained upon receipt / of the enclosed reply card, plus sixpence in stamps.

A / new line which we have recently developed is a skirt- / making service, from materials woven at our mills. The catalogue / contains details of styles and shades, and instructions for taking / correct measurements. These are designed to wear with the twin / sets.

We look forward to receiving an order from you / and can assure you of complete satisfaction.

Yours very truly, (300)

70 words per minute: (5 minutes):

Dear Sir,

We were pleased to receive your application for / membership of this club, and your fee for the current / year. A receipt is enclosed with your club card. Please / quote your membership number when ordering books.

May we draw / your attention to several additions to our book list? 'How / to Camp in Comfort' is a book which no camper / should be without. It is full of valuable hints on / all matters from choosing a suitable site to serving a / four-course meal with the minimum of equipment. There are / plenty of drawings and pictures to make it easy to / understand the instructions given, and the book is small enough / to slip with ease into a handbag or pocket. No / matter whether you are new to the camping game or / an old hand, this book will have something useful to / offer.

'New Guide to the British Isles' is a book / for the traveller, whether on foot or on wheels. Here / are clear maps of all parts of the country with / more than one hundred town plans. Information is given on / where to go, how to get there and what to / see on your way. Simply looking at this book will / make you long to set off on a trek or / a tour.

'Free for All' is another useful book for / holidays and weekends. It contains a list of all the / places which can be visited free of charge, with full / details of what may be seen at each and when / they are open.

All the above, or any books already / on our list may be obtained by you to read / or examine for seven days before you decide to purchase. / Those you want for your own are sold to you / at one-third less than the shop price. Do not / send any money with your order.

If you return the / books in good condition within a week, there will be / no charge. If you wish to retain the book, an / invoice will be sent to you during the second week. / You must buy one book every two months.

Yours truly, (350)

80 words per minute: (Two passages of 4 minutes each):

1. Everything is covered with snow, and it is still snowing. / There was snow yester-day, snow last night, and again snow / this morning. I shovel away at the snow to clear / a path, while still it snows. There is something futile / about moving snow; it is in great bulk, yet it / is light as nothing. It is like trying to throw / a feather.

When it is snowing or raining, so that / the children cannot go out, then it is a custom / that there shall be music in the drawing room, where / they are not usually allowed to play, so the room / becomes an exciting thing, a special treat for a wet / day, or a snowy one.

The snow gives me a / holiday, too; and a holiday, when you grow older, consists / in allowing yourself to take a long time doing a / thing which you usually do, if at all, in a / hurry.

But my holiday is brief, for with the snow / came the frost, and our talk is mostly about frozen / pipes. We must have water for ourselves and for the / animals, so the first job is to make a bonfire / round the pump in the yard to thaw that. Then / we remember the covered well, whose pump looks as if / it were one of the first products of the Iron / Age, like the first steam engine; its handle is old / and loose, but it works, like shaking a tired man / by the hand.

113

The animals are attended to first, and / their drinking troughs are thawed out. There is an old / copper boiler in the kitchen which must not be allowed / to go out, so fuel must be carried in. Cans / of hot water are rushed upstairs to release the frozen / taps in the bedroom and bathroom, while I warm the / waste pipes until the ice melts and the trapped water / rushes out and clears the icicles hanging from the spouts. (320)

2. Ladies and Gentlemen, a year ago in my Statement I / expressed the view that unless we had a major national / upset, the coming year should be quite favourable for us. / I am, therefore, very happy that this has proved to / be the case, and to report that we have achieved / an all-time record both in Group turnover and in / profits.

The Group net profit, after taxation, is up by / one hundred and fifty-five thousand, four hundred and thirty- / seven pounds to four hundred and fifty-two thousand, three / hundred and twenty-four pounds, and we have been able / to transfer the sum of two hundred thousand pounds to / the General Reserve Account.

With regard to our overseas companies / the year has been somewhat mixed. The results from our / South African company were poor, and we have taken steps / which will, I hope, ensure a satisfactory profit in future. / In my last report I referred to the measures we / had taken to improve the position of our Belgian Company, / and I am pleased to report that these were most / effective and a reasonable profit was made for the year / under review.

To predict the results of the year ahead / is always difficult, but with the present uncertain economic situation, / both at home and abroad, it is almost impossible. Costs / in labour and raw materials continue to increase and these / will be absorbed as far as possible by improved methods / of manufacture and increased sales. I believe the stability of / your Company lies in the variety of our products as / well as in the range of industries they serve. / So far this year the demand is holding at a / satisfactory level, and provided this continues I feel there should / be another successful year ahead with further improvement in our / trading position.

Once again I wish to record my appreciation / to the Staff and Employees for their continued loyal services. (320)

114

90 words per minute: (Two passages of 4 minutes each):

1. Probably no one man should have as many dogs in / his life as I have had, but there was more / pleasure than trouble in them for me, except in the / case of an Airedale, which we called Muggs. He gave / me more trouble than all the other fifty-five put / together.

As a matter of fact, he was not really / my dog; I came home from a holiday one summer / to find that my brother Roy had bought him while / I was away. A big, burly dog, he always acted / as if he thought I was not one of the / family. There was a slight advantage in being one of / the family, for he did not bite the family, as / often as he bit strangers.

We used to take turns / at feeding him to be in his good books, but / that did not always work. In the years that we / had him he bit everybody but mother, and he snapped / at her once, but missed. One day, because the dog / refused to chase rats in the pantry, mother slapped him / and he snapped at her, but missed. He was sorry / immediately, mother said. He was always sorry after he bit / someone, she said, but we could not see how she / made this out; he did not seem sorry to us. /

Mother used to send a box of candy every Christmas / to the people whom the dog bit. The list finally / contained forty or more names. Nobody could understand why we / did not get rid of the dog. I think that / one or two people tried to poison him, and a / retired army major fired at him once with his service / revolver, but Muggs lived to be almost eleven years old / and even when he could hardly get about he bit / a politician who had called to see my father on / business. My mother had never liked the politician - she said / he was not to be trusted - but she sent him / a box of candy that Christmas. He sent it right / back. Mother persuaded herself it was all for the best, / although father lost an important business connection because of it.

(360)

90 words per minute:

2. The thirty-first annual general meeting of Payne and Sons / Limited was held yesterday in Leicester, and the following is / an extract from the statement made by the Chairman.

115

The / turnover was the highest ever recorded in the history of / the company, but the pressure on margins made it difficult / to earn a reasonable profit. On the 17th September last, / I referred to the increases in almost all items of / our costs, which made it difficult to forecast the year's / results, but as you will see from the accounts the / figures for the complete year are better than would have / been forecast in September.

As the final dividend now proposed / was declared prior to the 3rd May, it can be / paid without having to account to the Revenue for the / tax deducted. This has been taken into account in recommending / the payment of the same total dividend as was made / for the previous year. Looking further to the future, our / dividend policy will have to be governed not only by / the amount of profit earned, but also by the effect / of Corporation Tax at the present rate of forty per / cent.

Your directors have given a great deal of time / and thought to the development of existing products and to / the search for new ones. This has, of course, involved / the company in heavy expenditure, but it is felt that / the cost is justified by your Board's policy of expansion / beyond our more traditional lines.

There does not seem to / be any prospect of costs coming down since we now / have to face an increase in steel prices which will / bring in its train many other increases.

The Company is / encouraged, however, by the fact that since the start of / the current year, the value of orders booked by all / our subsidiary companies shows a substantial increase over the same / period of the year under review. This is particularly welcome / because it is only by greater volume and increased efficiency / that higher costs can be covered. If this trend continues / it is reasonable to expect that profits for the current / year will be as good as those for last year. (360)

100 words per minute: (Two passages of 4 minutes each):

1. We had two doctors in our village when I was / a child, and the one who attended us lived in / the house next door. He was a tall, rather quiet / man, who had a passion for local history and plenty / of time to give to it.

One of the front / rooms of his large white house was used as an / office, which was cluttered up with stuffed birds, books and / papers. Here he received patients who were

116

able to consult /⁸⁰ him at home, thus saving half-a-crown or more, /⁹⁰ since his personal visits cost from five to ten shillings /¹⁰⁰ each, depending on the distance.

When the decision to call /¹¹⁰ the doctor had been made and the time of his /¹²⁰ arrival drew near, a solemn silence fell upon our household. /¹³⁰ Those of us, who were well, watched from the dining- /¹⁴⁰ room window. The patient, if it was summer, was lying /¹⁵⁰ in the four-poster bed in the spare room upstairs; /¹⁶⁰ if it was winter, he or she was in our /¹⁷⁰ small downstairs bedroom or on a cot in the living /¹⁸⁰ room. In either case the bed was spotless with fresh /¹⁹⁰ linen, and my mother was spotless also in a starched /²⁰⁰ white apron. No one spoke. The slow, heavy ticking of /²¹⁰ the clock was the only sound. All eyes were on /²²⁰ the doctor's house, awaiting the moment when he would leave /²³⁰ it with my father, who had gone to fetch him, /²⁴⁰ and enter ours.

When the doctor preceded my father through /²⁵⁰ the hall into the dining room, he paid no attention /²⁶⁰ to us children, though our eyes were fixed upon him. /²⁷⁰ What went on by the bedside we never knew, nor /²⁸⁰ do I think we were really interested. It was the /²⁹⁰ unusual presence of the doctor in our house which made /³⁰⁰ us dumb.

We remained very subdued in voice and manner /³¹⁰ for quite some time after the doctor had gone through /³²⁰ our gate and on towards his own house. We could /³³⁰ not easily resume our usual habits and we were not /³⁴⁰ too interested, I fear, in the fate of the patient. /³⁵⁰ I remember that I secretly hoped to be sent upon /³⁶⁰ some errand to the village so that I could answer /³⁷⁰ seriously all the many questions which I knew I should /³⁸⁰ be asked, repeating my mother's remark to us that 'all /³⁹⁰ was as well as it could be under the circumstances'. (400)

100 words per minute:

2. In the course of his speech, the Chairman said:

Towards /¹⁰ the end of the year under review we completed plans /²⁰ for the reorganisation of one of our cotton spinning mills, /³⁰ and placed contracts for the installation of the most modern /⁴⁰ machinery. When the new plant is complete and running on /⁵⁰ a three-shift basis, our productive efficiency will be so /⁶⁰ improved that we shall be able to maintain our present /⁷⁰ output from fewer machines and a reduced labour force. We /⁸⁰ hope that the scheme will be completed in about twelve / months' time, and the increased profit should be reflected in / the results for the year ending 30th June, nineteen hundred / and sixty-eight.

During the year under review we have / purchased additional plant for the manu-facture of Tyre Cord. This / will increase our productive capacity and so enable us to / meet immediate demands, but will still fall far short of / what I anticipate will be required from us in the / near future. In order to meet this further demand we / have recently completed plans for the expansion of this section. / I am pleased to be able to tell you that / the Board of Trade have expressed their approval of the / scheme and have issued the necessary Industrial Development certificate.

In / addition to all this, we are trying to bring our / Canvas Section up to date. The looms we have in / mind run at much higher speeds than those at present / in use and consequently the output per unit will be / greatly increased. I hope we shall be able to complete / these plans during the current year.

The foregoing plans, which / involve the purchase of new machinery and the con-struction of / new buildings, will require a capital expenditure of over one / million pounds. This figure is in itself a clear indication / of our confidence in the future.

The many improvements which / I have outlined in this statement should enable us to / cope with the increased pressure on margins which the industry / has experienced during recent years. The results of this development / programme will be progressive and some benefit should be apparent / in the figures for the current year; nevertheless, it will / probably be a further two years before all sections are / completed. While emphasis may change, and we must be prepared / as always to change with it, I am convinced that / the demand for our specialised products will continue to expand. (400)